COUNSELLING

Liz Hodgkinson

SIMON & SCHUSTER

LONDON·SYDNEY·NEW YORK·TOKYO·SINGAPORE·TORONTO

First published in Great Britain by
Simon & Schuster Ltd in 1992
A Paramount Communications Company

Simon & Schuster Ltd
West Garden Place
Kendal Street
London W2 2AQ

Simon & Schuster of Australia Pty Ltd
Sydney

A CIP catalogue record for this book is
available from the British Library
ISBN 0–671–71046–X

Typeset in Garamond ITC by Goodfellow & Egan, Cambridge
Printed and bound in Great Britain by
Billing & Sons Ltd, Worcester

Contents

Acknowledgements

For expert help in preparing this book, the author would like to thank Judith Baron of the British Association for Counselling, The Rev. Derek Blows of the Westminster Pastoral Foundation, The Bristol Cancer Help Centre and counsellor Jenny Bateman.

Introduction

You've probably heard of counselling. In fact, it would be strange if you hadn't heard of it, as the word is now cropping up all over the place.

For instance, you may have gone to see your doctor recently and found that, as well as the practice nurse and the receptionist, there is now a more mysterious person called a 'counsellor' installed as well. Your child may have had a problem at school and been referred to the 'school counsellor' – a personage who certainly never existed when you were a kid. Or maybe your college-aged son or daughter has had difficulties with exams or personal relationships and has been advised to see the 'counsellor' – an individual whose job it is, apparently, to help the students sort out their lives and emotions. If you, or colleagues, have been suffering from stress at work, you may now be asked to see the 'stress counsellor'.

Perhaps you've even got a friend who is considering becoming a counsellor, or you know somebody who is already training as one. Look in any newspaper nowadays and you will see advertisements for counsellors and counselling courses.

With all this, you may be wondering just what counselling is about, and who these counsellors are – some new kind of shrink, or old do-gooders in a different guise? Can they help you – or are they just interfering busybodies? And if they can help, just what kind of assistance might they offer?

This book has been written to try to answer all the

awkward questions people now have about counselling, for although we may know the word, most of us would hesitate to describe exactly what counselling is, or what counsellors are supposed to do. And, it must be said, many of us are highly suspicious, secretly wondering whether counselling is some vast and unnecessary job-creation scheme.

Not long ago, I too was extremely suspicious of anything which smacked of counselling. In my ignorance, I considered those calling themselves counsellors were basically untrained, fussy do-gooders who could tell me no more about myself than I knew already. I associated the word counselling with terms such as 'caring' and 'supportive' – terms which have become so overused that they have lost much of their original positive meaning, yet acquired the power to annoy.

But then I had some counselling myself – and the experience altered my attitude completely. I agreed, somewhat reluctantly, to counselling sessions simply because they were offered when I was working on a journalistic assignment at a therapy centre. I was only agreeing, I told myself, so that I would be better equipped to understand what it was all about. I certainly didn't consider that I *needed* counselling in any way. Why, I was a perfectly sane, sensible and rational person who could sort out my own problems, thank you very much, without the help of some 'caring' counsellor. Whatever could a mere counsellor, a stranger, tell me about myself that I didn't know already?

But the counselling sessions were a revelation. I began to realize for the first time that, far from being the invulnerable self-knowledgable person I had supposed, in fact for most of my adult life I had been blocking off important emotions, not allowing myself to feel, that I had been badly hurt in the past and had been denying this hurt. I had operated a survival mechanism which was no longer serving me well. My counselling sessions helped me to understand this – and to emerge a nicer, more positive and more emotionally complete person. The transformation and self-understanding which resulted could not, I believe, have happened without the counselling.

Oh yes, the sceptical might scoff. Counsellors may be very good at telling us about our hidden motives, our blocked traumas, our repressed childhoods – but isn't it all making a mountain out of a molehill? Surely, as adults, we should just get on with our lives, forget about what happened in the past, and not try to drag it all back up? Isn't it better to let sleeping dogs lie, and not dwell on what might have happened to us at the age of three? Isn't there altogether too much of this soul-searching about these days?

Certainly I had this attitude once – before I went for counselling. What I can say now is that counselling can give people insights into themselves which they did not have before, and enable them to understand patterns in their lives, which puts them more in charge of what happens to them and less caught up in a remorseless wheel of events. And counsellors, I discovered, do *not* exist to advise you what to do or tell you, for example, that you were secretly in love with your father, that you had a repressed childhood, that you have always looked for love, that you have low self-esteem. What they do is provide a setting where you can realize these and other things for yourself, and make your own decisions about what you do.

I learned from personal experience that, at its best, counselling can help us to see ourselves more positively, put events into a clearer perspective and come to terms with negative emotions such as blame and guilt. It was these positive experiences, after my initial scepticism, which encouraged me to research the whole subject from the lay person's point of view. I am not a counsellor and my aim in this book is to provide as objective a picture as possible of counselling, although I start from personal knowledge of how beneficial it can be. I also know from my researches that most people who have gone for counselling (often rather reluctantly or with misgivings, as I did) have felt their lives were overwhelmingly changed for the better once they had taken the plunge.

Just recently, I was talking to a colleague who had almost died in a fire in a Cairo hotel during an all-expenses-paid trip to Egypt to launch a new perfume. The occupant of the next bedroom, a twenty-nine-year-old freelance journalist with a small daughter, had perished in the flames. Two women died; several occupants of the hotel were badly injured.

All of the survivors, tough, assertive journalists and editors, were offered trauma counselling after the event. Some took it up, others felt they would prefer to manage without. A year later, it became clear, said my colleague, that those who had gone for counselling had been much better able to come to terms with the event, with the emotions that it had stirred up for them. Most of those who had not, by contrast, were still deeply troubled by the tragedy and continued to relive it in their dreams and nightmares. They still felt terrible guilt over being survivors when others had died, compounded by the fact that a basically trivial pleasure trip had had such a horrifying outcome.

My colleague found that the tragedy triggered buried emotions from the past and called her whole life into question. 'I was amazed that I started thinking about certain aspects of my childhood, that all my life I had been terrified of being trapped in a place I couldn't get out of, and that my worst fears were realized. I couldn't open the window of the hotel, and I screamed and screamed.' She said, 'I learned that this event wasn't just something awful that happened in isolation, but that it touched on all kinds of deep emotions about myself, my parents, my relationships, my job, my values. Everything had to be re-evaluated in the light of this experience, and put into a new perspective. I don't think I could have done it without the help of an experienced trauma counsellor.'

But although most people I know who have been for

counselling say they are glad they did, the majority have not known in advance what they were letting themselves in for. It is because counselling remains such an unknown quantity for many of us that it is surrounded by fears and doubts. I hope that this book will go some way towards dispelling those fears by informing people about counselling, how it operates, how it grew up, and what it can and can't do for you.

It is written from the viewpoint that counselling is basically a good thing, a positive movement, and that if carried out sensitively and expertly, it can heal both emotional and physical distress. It is also written in the belief that, for most of us, there are times in our lives when we may need some outside input, a detached, yet sympathetic relationship, to enable us to see a troubling situation in a new and more helpful light. This assumes that our feelings are better not kept to ourselves but brought out into the open, with a trusted person in a safe setting. For it is increasingly realized that the stiff upper lip, grin and bear it attitude is not necessarily helpful, or conducive to self-knowledge and good relationships. I believe that counselling can help us to understand ourselves and our motives, to stop denying aspects of ourselves and start admitting the truth. It can enable us to come to terms with the pain of separation, divorce, bereavement, job or money losses, accidents – all the experiences that may be difficult to face alone.

But although, through personal experience and research, I have come to believe that the counselling movement is something positive, to be encouraged and welcomed rather than sneered at and dismissed, this does not mean that I think everything in the counselling world is rosy. For example, anybody at all can at the moment quite legally set up as a counsellor, without any training whatever, for, unlike a doctor or an architect, a counsellor does not have to have specific qualifications. Moreover, the term counselling has a broad meaning and includes a variety of approaches and methods. This leaves many traps for the unwary, for those who don't know much about the subject – which is, after all, most of us. How can we know a 'good' counsellor, somebody who is right for us? Also, there are professionally accepted boundaries within which counsellors operate and you may have no idea whether a particular counsellor may be exceeding these boundaries, or may indeed be hindering rather than helping.

This book aims to tell you what you can expect from counselling, what it is designed to do, and how you can decide whether counselling might be for you. It tells you about the different types of counselling that are available, and the qualities and training to expect from counsellors. It gives advice on finding the right kind of counselling for you, with practical information about time and money, plus a list of counselling sources. My hope is that the book will go some way to clearing the confusion which now surrounds the subject of counselling for many people, and that it will provide a helpful consumer's guide to the whole movement as it stands at present.

1

What Exactly is Counselling?

So popular has counselling become these days that it has been called one of the major growth industries of our time. And certainly, increasingly, it does seem as though we can't live our lives without some kind of counselling being suggested.

At one time you saw the doctor in the surgery. Now, you may be referred to a counsellor, particularly if you are suffering from an illness which may be defined as 'stress-related'. Whatever difficulty you may encounter, in your personal life, at work, socially, it seems you can no longer tackle it yourself, you have to be counselled as well. In fact, so prevalent has counselling become that it may appear as if counsellors lie in wait at every turn to trap the unwary, the hesitant or confused. This was brought home by a *Private Eye* cartoon, where a man was seen rushing through a crowd of people gathered round a road accident victim. 'Let me through!' he screamed. 'I'm a grief counsellor!'

The word 'counselling' has certainly entered the language – along with much scepticism about what this activity is, its helpfulness, and just what the qualifications are of those setting themselves up as counsellors to the rest of us.

So what exactly *is* counselling – and who are these ever-increasing numbers of people who are offering themselves at every turn as counsellors? What do they know that the rest of us don't? How is it that they can help us get over a crisis better than we can manage on our own? Do we really need them, and just what are they doing? Surely we used to manage perfectly well, or at least well enough, on our own.

So What Is Counselling?

At its most simple, counselling is talking about your problems with someone outside your own circle who is there to listen to you, with the idea that this will help you feel better able to cope with life. This may not sound that much different from having a heart-to-heart chat with a friend or family member and, indeed, many people look no further than their own circle for support at a difficult time. But for many other people, there may be no friends or family to turn to or, very often, they feel this is precisely where they can't turn.

One trouble with talking to friends and family about your problems is that they may not understand your anxiety and distress; they may tell you to 'snap out of it' or that you should have got over the difficulty by now. You may feel you can't burden them any more, that the problem is too much for them as well as for you.

Also, most friends and families have a vested interest in keeping you as you are and they may not want you to change. For instance, a man who drinks heavily will more often than not have other drinkers as his friends. Like attracts like. If this man decides to become teetotal, he may find that these friends will try to persuade him to have a drink – just one, be one of the lads, have a bit of fun. Never mind that his drinking is ruining his life. To them, his drying out means loss of the friend they know; after all, it was the drinking that brought them together.

If you're single, you will tend to have single friends; if you're married, most of your friends and social acquaintances are likely to be couples. Should you announce you intend to change your state, you may well find those 'friends' melt away. On the whole, people want you to be as they are – and don't respect your choice to be something different. A newly divorced person, for example, is often told by married friends, 'Oh, you'll soon find someone else'. To respect that person's single position would mean that they were no longer all in the same boat.

Families can be even more tied in to maintaining the status quo and where problems are directly connected with family relationships, it may seem impossible to talk about them with a family member or feel that you are understood if you do. Even if the problem has no apparent family connection, for example job redundancy, in talking about it we can quickly become tangled up in strong emotions that are hard to unravel with someone closely connected to us.

The difference, though, is not simply about talking to an 'outsider' rather than someone you know. For this outsider, the counsellor, is there specifically to concentrate on your difficulties and give you, as the client, an opportunity to talk freely, in confidence, about your thoughts and feelings in a way not possible with friends or family. Counsellors are not only people detached from your daily life but people who are, above all, trained to listen. And listening, in the counselling sense, is not merely lending a sympathetic ear but is a creative act. It involves giving you as the client full attention, without imposing judgments, bringing in the counsellors' life stories or telling you what they think you should do.

This does not mean that counsellors don't talk but that their responses are concentrated on clarifying what you are saying and feeling. There should be no attempt by them to socialize you back into a traditional role or to 'cure' you of your attitudes or beliefs. The aim is not to give specific advice but to help you discover what you want out of life, to put you in charge, to help you become autonomous and independent and less at the mercy of others or your own emotions.

The British Association for Counselling (BAC), which

began life in 1977 with the aim of setting the whole counselling movement on a more professional basis, states: 'The task of counselling is to give the client an opportunity to explore, discover and clarify ways of living more resourcefully and towards greater well-being.' As Adrienne Saunderson, a counsellor with Relate (formerly Marriage Guidance) for some twenty years, puts it:

> Counselling can be defined as a process through which one person, the counsellor, helps another person, the client or patient, to express thoughts and feelings in such a way as to clarify difficulties and come to terms with some new experience, thereby facing the problem with renewed confidence.

In general, counselling addresses two main issues, change and loss, which is why it is likely to be on offer or recommended whenever there is some turning-point in life, something which may constitute a major crisis or challenge. The purpose of counselling is to help people facing these crises come to terms with them, cope with them, and develop strategies for living their lives to the full afterwards.

Its aim is not to give specific advice but to help you discover what you, as the client, want out of life, to put you in charge, to help you become independent. It is all about empowerment of the individual, helping people to take responsibility for their actions and be less at the mercy of others or their own emotions.

Counselling is there to give us a helping hand whenever life becomes difficult, when we may be fuddled and bewildered because of overwhelming emotion, stress or trauma. Although theoretically it can address just about any difficulty, in practice it is rarely an option for those suffering severe psychiatric disorders, among other reasons because of the demands it makes of the client and the training limitations of the counsellor. But it can be, and often is, of benefit to those who are recovering from a breakdown – or fear either the recurrence or onset of one.

Crises, turning-points in life, indefinable emotional problems, these are what counselling addresses. No, we don't have to have it and, yes, we probably could manage somehow on our own. But with counselling we should be able to manage better.

Who are the Counsellors?

Who are these people who can supposedly help us to manage better, who have set themselves to help us? What is so special about them that they apparently know things we don't?

The word counsel in its original sense meant 'wise advice' and counsellors were considered to be people who had more wisdom than ordinary folk. Counsellors today would probably stress that they are not there to give specific advice of any kind, nor would they make claims to be naturally more wise than others. They are people like you or me — but they have travelled just a little further along the road to self-knowledge, to self-actualization, to use a Sixties term. They are people who have personally experienced pain and have had to look hard at themselves, face up to the reality of their difficulties and cope with them. They are thus in a better position (according to the theory) to understand what others might be going through.

Counsellors who specialize in particular kinds of difficulties are often people who have undergone similar problems themselves. Thus, those who undertake cancer counselling, for instance, may well have fought cancer themselves. Those who offer abortion or bereavement counselling have often experienced searing loss and overwhelming grief themselves. They have grown and learned — and are passing on the benefits of their greater understanding to others.

The counsellors' experiences, however, may well be quite different from those of their clients — in any case, no two people's experiences are ever the same – and counsellors are not expected to have suffered similar traumas to their clients in order for them to understand. But they are expected to be people who, for whatever reason, have looked inside themselves, faced their own problems and have, to some extent, arrived at serenity and understanding, and a more positive perspective. If not, then they have no right to be practising as counsellors.

Counsellors should be people who not only offer these personal qualities but who have also been fully trained to put them at the benefit of their clients. In going to a counsellor, you have no guarantee that she or he will be trained since it is perfectly legal to practise as a counsellor without any training at all. Some people would even claim that good counsellors are born, not made – and certainly experience can count for a lot. Nor can training guarantee a good counsellor. But having said that, training is seen as increasingly important and the BAC is now trying very hard to establish high professional standards of training.

More will be said later in the book about the many kinds of counsellor training courses that have burgeoned recently. Essentially, training means that counsellors are required to look very closely at themselves, their motivations, feelings, experiences, and to learn, besides theory, the skills for enabling others to look into themselves. The emphasis is on counsellors reaching a high level of self-awareness, so that they don't become blindly caught up in their clients' feelings and are able to put their problems into perspective, look at them clearly.

Counsellors are, above all, trained to listen, to give their full attention to the other person. As the BAC defines it, counselling is 'when a person, occupying regularly or temporarily the role of counsellor, offers or agrees explicitly to give time, attention and respect to another person temporarily in the role of client'. Time, attention and respect – these are the key services counsellors offer, and ones which it may be difficult to command in everyday life. But in the counselling relationship, they are what you should expect, and have a right to demand.

But counsellors are fallible human beings like anybody else, not gurus or founts of all knowledge and wisdom. They should not be looked up to as some kind of oracle, dispensing divine words. They do not and cannot offer instant solutions, they do not necessarily have the answers.

There is a popular image of counsellors being people who can make us better. We may imagine that counselling can provide some kind of 'miracle cure' – when it can't. Counsellors are not there to 'cure' or 'rescue'. Clients must come to their own conclusions, lead their own lives. At their best, counsellors can help us find the confidence and self-esteem needed to break free from our past, to have the courage to change and develop, to become more of our own person and not just a sheep following the herd. They won't normally delve deep into the unconscious but they will support clients while self-explorations are being made, will provide intellectual clarification and attention to the presenting problem.

Counsellors have a particular role to play in helping individuals find their own autonomy and strength, and those who set themselves up as counsellors should be neutral, non-judgmental, able to respect the choices you are making and help you come to your own conclusions. They are not – or should not be – there to tell you what to do, to make your choices for you.

People who see counselling as a cop-out for the weak and the dependent, who think of counsellors as do-gooding sympathizers who are encouraging self-pity and self-indulgence, have got a mistaken view of what it's about. It requires personal courage to admit: I need help, I can't manage on my own. And it takes courage to admit: I may have been wrong, I may have made choices which were not in my own or others' best interests. Counsellors are people who have, in theory at least, taken that step and are there to help us find the even greater courage needed to make our own choices and take responsibility for them.

How Counselling Grew Up

Counselling in its modern sense has been developing since the 1960s and grew out of the American 'human potential movement', which was all about personal growth. At its heart, the counselling movement believes that every one of life's challenges, such as job loss, divorce, bereavement, illness, can be seen as a starting point for growth, change and greater insight. We can 'grow', according to the beliefs of the counselling movement, when we are able to learn more about ourselves from the painful lessons of the past and emerge with renewed strength and self-confidence.

The ways that we are believed to achieve this growth owe much to the idea of the 'talking cure', which began in a systematic way with Freudian analysis at the end of the nineteenth century. At that time, the idea of having somebody to listen to you, to interpret your dreams and to help you come to some conclusion about your life through free association of ideas, through bringing repressed child-hood traumas to the conscious level, was quite new and revolutionary.

In the main, the purpose of traditional analysis was to help people face and release repressed traumas, usually ones which related back to their childhood. Patients would lie on the couch as they spoke and the analyst would be seated behind them, out of sight, and become a disembodied voice. As time went on, different schools of psychoanalysis were formed and a whole new language grew up to describe certain mental or emotional states — words such as repression, resistance, projection, introjec-tion, all acquired new meanings in relation to psychoana-lytic theory.

Modern counselling has developed out of psychoana-lytic theories and practices but it works very differently and today bears very little relation to anything Freud would have recognized. Nowadays, few counsellors – or analysts – would talk in terms of a 'cure'. After initial misplaced confidence in the ability of the 'talking cure' actually to cure, there is a much more humble recognition of what counselling and psychotherapy (in America, what we know as counselling is usually termed psychotherapy and the terms are in many respects interchangeable) can actually achieve.

To talk about your feelings, about your experiences of life, both past and present, is still, however, what counselling (and other therapies) are largely about. Counselling is still often referred to as a talking cure, even though cure would generally be accepted as much too radical a word; rather, a healing process is considered to take place through talking of feelings to a listener who can provide a special quality of response.

One indication of how counselling has developed its own ethos is that in the counselling relationship those coming for help are referred to as clients rather than patients. This in itself implies that they are seen more as equals rather than as sick people coming to the expert for a cure. They do not lie on a couch, which puts them in a different kind of relationship to the listener, but usually sit on a chair facing the counsellor, making eye-to-eye contact. The client is considered the 'expert' on her- or himself and the counsellor's main job is to be a 'facilitator', to bring out what the client really feels and wants, and help him or her to live more fully in future.

In trying to help the client in this way, counsellors may make use of theories of the unconscious mind and childhood development as elaborated through psychology – but the counselling movement developed to get away from any fixed theories, any one school of analytical thought, and counsellors will avoid using theoretical labels. The individual is all important. The importance of childhood experiences are always taken into account but, unlike analysis or intensive psychotherapy, counselling does not aim to delve deep into such past experiences or try to explore the recesses of the unconscious mind.

In contrast, counselling tends to concentrate on the 'here and now', on the problem itself, believing that with the help of a counsellor, clients themselves have the ability to search for and find their own truth. It is considered that present problems can often be resolved without going too painfully and lengthily into the past.

The counselling movement also developed in response to the elitist limitations of analysis. Because of it being so time-consuming and costly, it could reach only a very small number of affluent, leisured people, excluding many others who could, theoretically at least, benefit from it. There was a pressing need for a more cost-effective way of helping people to come to terms with their problems and difficulties.

Out of this came counselling's emphasis on a more focused approach, goal-oriented and working to a more or less fixed time-scale, rather than the more open-ended exploration of analysis, which might continue at four or five sessions a week over many years. Also out of this came a move away from the hierarchical and patriarchal inheritance of psychoanalysis, which placed such power in the hands of the (usually male) analyst, and towards an attitude of greater equality and open-mindedness.

Why Do We Need So Much Counselling?

Counselling is, as we have seen, a relatively new phenomenon, growing up only since the 1960s. So why do we suddenly all need it so badly? However did we manage with our feelings, our pain and anxiety, our conflicts and distress, before counsellors appeared on the scene?

The reason we need counselling is because, increasingly, we can't seem to manage well on our own. It is a moot point whether we ever did but certainly there is far more loss and change in life than at any other time in history.

In the past, of course, terrible things did happen, but in the main, life was relatively stable. People usually had support systems around them – the extended family, the village, the community. Now, more and more, we are on our own. More people are living on their own, more are getting divorced, moving to other countries, changing jobs, changing careers – all things which either did not happen in the past, or not to very many people.

As consultant cardiologist Peter Nixon put it: 'We started off this century with windpower and horsepower, and now we send people into space, can travel thousands of miles in just a few hours – and our bodies and minds simply can't cope with these rapid changes.'

There is more choice and change than ever before. In the past, there were few choices available to a woman, other than marriage – and then little control of whether she had children or not. And most men did not have the opportunity to change jobs or careers. Although Dickens' novels are full of stories about people experiencing terrible changes, losses and reversals in their lives, the fact was that life, for most people, had very little change in it. The fictionalized autobiography of Flora Thompson, *Lark Rise to Candleford*, gives a picture of how predictable life was in the past; hardly anybody, rich or poor, in her story had an opportunity to escape from their background, upbringing or circumstances.

Very few families in the past broke up and lived apart. This is not to say that it was better, or worse, but when there is very little choice available, then there is little scope for, or point in, counselling – except, perhaps, to try to make people more content with their lot. This was the job of religion in the past – God bless the squire and his relations, and keep us in our proper stations, was the message of most clergymen (the forerunners of counsellors) to those who were dissatisfied with their lot in life.

And you can see that there would not be a lot of mileage in personal growth if people weren't free to do anything but live their lives exactly as before.

It is no accident that the counselling movement has grown up at the same time as we are increasingly faced with often bewildering choices in our lives. Nowadays, the average – not just the rich or leisured – woman in the West can choose to travel, to work abroad, to marry or not, to have children or not, or to have children and bring them up as a single parent. She can choose to have a career and no children, she can combine a career with having children, or she can have children and not go out to work; she can delay having children until her career is off the ground, she can get divorced, live as a lesbian, alone, with her parents or thousands of miles away from them. She can have abortions, be sterilized, take professional qualifications at any age, change her career.

Men don't have to make the same dramatic decisions concerning childbirth, of course, although they will be affected by them – but they also have far more choices available regarding their personal and work lives. There are now many more opportunities than ever before for both men and women to fulfil their personal potential – a luxury the majority could never even consider when most of life had to be lived between tramlines laid down by others.

There are also far fewer moral and ethical guidelines. In the past, we 'knew' that sex before marriage was wrong, that having children out of wedlock was wrong. We turned to religion for guidance, had its teachings to follow. Now, only a minority have firm religious beliefs on which they base their lives, and many of society's traditional values have been questioned. Just when life poses us with so many challenges, we have often lost the inner means to cope with them.

The sheer amount of choice available to more people these days means that we have to take more responsibility for our actions. We can't (although we often do) put the blame on other people or 'society' for what we do, who we marry — or don't, whether we stay at home, move, live abroad. We are (with a few exceptions) free to marry the person of our choice, to travel, to work abroad. Some choices were never available to our grandparents' generations, such as easy credit facilities, enabling us to buy expensive things we can't really afford — houses, cars, foreign holidays. We can choose to have all these things, and they seem easy, even free. But, always, there is a price to pay for exercising that choice. Borrowing money can mean getting into ever bigger and more worrying debt and having to pay extortionate interest rates.

With so many choices and changes, things can much more easily go out of control. House prices may tumble, interest rates soar, inflation wipe out the real value of a lifetime's savings. In addition to natural disasters such as famine and earthquakes, we now have air crashes and hi-jacking, nuclear plants exploding, international terrorism. Far-away wars are brought into our living rooms as they are happening, in graphic and bloody detail. We can no longer ignore what is happening on the other side of the world, in places we have never visited.

The trouble is that many of us just don't have the means to cope with any of the rapid changes that are happening in our lives, let alone sudden disasters. Often we feel expected to cope on our own, just when we most need support. Families may either not be there, or they don't understand. In fact, nowadays, we often need help in order to be able to cope *with* our families — it's no accident that the book co-authored by comedian John Cleese called *Families and How to Survive them* has been a bestseller for several years.

We need help — but who do we turn to? This is where counsellors come in. Those in the counselling movement believe that increasingly, we need help with 'life skills' — things which we may have fondly, and mistakenly, imagined came easily and without effort.

Counselling has grown at such a fast pace because there is an insatiable demand for it. Although it may seem as if every other person is now a counsellor of some kind, the fact is that there aren't anything like enough counsellors to cope with the people who are requesting their services. For instance, anybody wanting to see a Relate (Marriage Guidance) counsellor may have to wait several months. Counsellors are not sitting waiting for customers, not rushing to poke their noses into your business. Most have workloads they can hardly manage – and more and more people are asking for their services.

Types of counselling

One of the reasons for the mystery still surrounding counselling is that there are many different types of counselling, each of which grew out of a particular theory of how the mind works or how individuals are adapting to their present society. The names given to types of counselling tend to make it sound esoteric and almost like a religion. In fact, they are just labels which indicate methods by which certain counsellors work.

Most counselling courses concentrate on a particular type of counselling, based on a certain theory. For instance, some take as their starting point the belief that we all started off innocent, loving, peaceful and enthusiastic but that we have become negative, fearful and hostile through bad early experiences. According to this theory, we can all become peaceful, loving and confident once we let go of outdated scripts and learn to love again.

Yet other schools of counselling adhere to the belief that as we grew up, we learned certain bad habits of behaviour. Counselling here can teach us to replace these bad habits with good ones. (Of course, what constitutes a 'good' rather than a 'bad' habit will depend on the views held by the founder of that particular theory of human behaviour.)

We shall be looking more closely at how these various schools of thought have affected different counselling methods in a later chapter. To name some of them here, you may come across person-centred counselling, psycho-dynamic counselling, gestalt counselling, behavioural counselling, transactional analysis counselling and psycho-synthesis counselling.

Confused? Don't be. When it comes down to it, there is far less difference between these different types than their names at first suggest. Whatever the theories behind particular schools of thought, all counselling has as its basic aim empowerment of the individual and a replacing of low self-esteem and lack of a sense of identity by a strong, positive attitude, belief in oneself, and enhanced self-confidence.

To Sum Up

Counselling, as defined by the BAC, is

> the skilled and principled use of relationship to facilitate self-knowledge, emotional acceptance and growth in the optimal development of personal resources. The overall aim is to provide an opportunity to work towards living more satisfactorily and resourcefully. Counselling relation-ships will vary according to need but may be concerned with the developmental issues, addressing and resolving specific problems, making decisions, coping with crises, developing personal insights and knowledge, working through feelings of inner conflict or improving relation-ships with others.

At its best, counselling facilitates the most exciting journey any individual can make – the journey of self-discovery. Counselling sessions give you the time, the space and the opportunity to discover things about your-self that might otherwise remain hidden. In a safe setting, where you won't be judged, you can explore exactly where you are at, why you are where you are, what you can do to make life better and more meaningful in the future and how you can come to terms with your past, mistakes and all.

Essentially, counselling is a branch of healing. It is about excising negative thoughts and stopping feeling bad about yourself; it is to help people bring the whole of their lives into harmony rather than being fragmented.

Counselling is a voluntary activity; nobody can make you go, or continue. And unless it is undertaken willingly, it is very unlikely to help. To go for counselling means having the courage to admit that you are in difficulties, that you do not have all the answers, but that you are prepared to look hard at your life and where you are going, and make changes if necessary.

Counselling is hard work and won't painlessly melt away your problems. To benefit from it requires motivation, dedication and a willingness to really look at yourself, your own attitudes, to take responsibility for what you have done and are going to do, and to stop being a victim. It is rarely an easy path because it may require attempting to change long-ingrained habits of thinking.

Counsellors can't wave magic wands, turn back the clock, undo what has been done, but they do make it possible for you to face up to problems in life and tackle them with renewed vigour and strength. To help in this way, counsellors need to have certain qualities. Although it may be that some people are more 'natural' counsellors than others, the consensus of opinion now is that nobody can become a truly effective counsellor without undergoing a period of specific training and being willing themselves to be in therapy and supervision.

But however important the counsellor's qualities are, it is the client who does the real work. Psychologist Windy Dryden, of Goldsmith's College, London, and the author of many books on counselling theory and practice, says that there is a feeling that counselling is responsible for huge and consistent beneficial changes in clients. In fact, he points out, successful counselling has happened where the client has been able to make changes of his or her own accord, changes which certainly may not have been possible without counselling but which come from the client, not the counsellor.

Although counselling may be available free in some organizations, and occasionally through the NHS or social services, it often involves some kind of payment. Private counsellors will certainly charge. But counselling won't be nearly as expensive as analysis or most psychotherapy, if only because much less time is involved. Counselling, too, is often seen as far less threatening than psychiatry or analysis because the client remains in charge.

At its best, counselling can certainly benefit people and provide a bridge to help them from one way of life to another, better and more effective one. At its worst, it may catapult people into making dramatic life changes before they are ready for them. In the next chapter you can find out if you feel you could benefit from counselling, whether this kind of 'talking cure' might be just what you, or possibly somebody among your family or friends, need at the moment.

2

Is Counselling for You?

The short answer to this probably is yes. It's likely that everybody – you, me, even counsellors themselves – can benefit from some kind of counselling. There are few people who can really manage on their own, who can face every life change and challenge with confidence and serenity, and without help or input of some kind.

Those with a religious faith may turn to God to clarify their position and attitude. But most of us have to choose the next best source available to us – human counsellors.

Anybody who is going through a severe life crisis, whether this is serious illness, bereavement, the loss of a job or close relationship, would probably find counselling helpful. Those who are undergoing great stress for whatever reason, and who cannot see easily which way to turn, may also benefit. Those who feel that their lives are just not going right, but can't quite put their finger on why or how, could also find professional counselling useful.

But you don't have to be at a major crossroads or impasse in your life, you don't have to be trying to cope with a severe trauma or life change, to feel that counselling might be for you. It is for anybody at all who feels that life could be improved, that self-esteem and self-confidence could be raised, that personal relationships could be more satisfactory – but who is experiencing difficulty in overcoming these challenges alone.

Counselling is an appropriate option for anybody suffering from anxiety or pain, or for whom life is generally not fulfilling. It will not provide an instant, magic solution to every one of life's difficulties, or ensure that no more problems ever crop up, but if carried out effectively, counselling will help you to cope better and put you back in charge of your own life.

Having said all that, counselling cannot work if the person doesn't want it. This is why, before ever considering counselling, you should consider very carefully what it might mean, what disruptions it could have, and how it could affect your job, relationships and place in society. There is always a danger that counselling could start off a process by which everything is turned on its head and certainly, after counselling, you will never be exactly the same again.

You have to ask yourself: do I seriously want to see my life and relationships with greater clarity; am I ready to make whatever changes I need to? Am I ready to deal with whatever pain might come up during counselling? Because you can be sure that, if it is effective, it will 'hit the spot' – that is, reveal something in yourself which has been hidden and which has been preventing you from making informed choices in your life.

Going for counselling may mean that you have to ask yourself – and answer – awkward questions. You may have to face things you've been putting off facing before, such as that your parents may not have been so altruistic, loving and giving as you fondly imagined, or wanted them to be. You may have to face the fact that you married the wrong person and for the wrong reasons. You may have to face up to the realization that you have been denying and resisting a lot of painful truths in your life. You may have to face unpleasant aspects of yourself which have formerly been buried. A voyage of self-discovery involves taking risks and re-evaluating all of your life. Unless it does so, it can be considered a waste of time.

But, you may say, counselling offers to help people come to terms with specific issues, such as redundancy, infertility, donating sperm, getting out of debt. How would talking through these specific issues bring in every aspect of life, and involve the pain of facing the truth?

The answer is that facing up to a specific difficulty always involves coming to terms with your attitudes and ideas in general. Nothing is confined to a single issue.

To give an example: nowadays, we are told, around one in six couples faces some kind of infertility problem. In present-day life, we have been led to believe that virtually whatever we want, we can have, without waiting. If we want a house, a car, a holiday, we can go to the bank and get the money for the purchase – never mind that we can't really afford the item at present. We have it, then we must pay – with interest.

In the old days, people got married and had children. Or they didn't. Either way, having children was largely outside individual control. Then family planning came along and showed us how to have just the children we wanted, when we wanted them. The result of this was that people expected to conceive the moment they decided to reproduce – and were aggrieved if conception didn't happen at the appointed time.

Then infertility began to be closely researched and exciting breakthroughs, such as fertility drugs, in-vitro fertilization, assisted conception, surrogate motherhood, were announced in the media. This made many people imagine that infertility could be cured and that they could just go and 'order' a baby. But of course, it doesn't work like that, and many people who want babies can't seem to have them.

On the face of it, it may seem that wanting a baby is a simple thing. After all, a baby is considered universally desirable, something which puts the seal on a loving relationship. We have the biological, fundamental urge to reproduce and why should we be denied it because of some technical problem?

That's how it sounds. But anybody who goes for infertility counselling may well find that highly complicated factors are uncovered in this apparently simple human wish to reproduce. Women 'desperately' wanting to conceive may be asked to consider: *why* do you so desperately want a baby? What is lacking in your life that you imagine a baby will fulfil? Do you actually like children? If so, have you ever considered adopting, fostering, or even taking children on holiday? Have you ever considered working with children, perhaps in a children's home?

Do you feel that a baby might bind your marriage together? Stop your husband from straying? Do you want a baby because you feel you will make a better parent than your own parents? Do you want to show them how to do it? Do you want a baby because you are the only woman on your estate without one?

Do you believe that people with children are happier than those without? If so, why is there so much child abuse and ill-treatment about? Have you considered the question of overpopulation? Do you want a baby because you believe it is your right — or because you believe that you could offer a truly loving, nurturing home to another human being?

Do you want to have a baby just to show the world you can? To get out of taking responsibility for earning a living? To have someone take care of you in your old age? Have you ever thought of fulfilling your own potential, rather than taking responsibility for another person? Why do you think you would make a good parent? And so on.

With every question that may be raised by a counsellor, the woman is being asked to look deep into her heart, to ask herself searching questions about her motivations. They may not be what she has imagined. People usually become very sad and bitter when they can't conceive but until counselling became an integral part of fertility services, few had ever asked themselves exactly why they were so desperate to bring another life into the world.

This is just one example of how an apparently simple issue is revealed through counselling to have many aspects. The idea is to enable clearer thinking and greater emotional awareness in order to plan an effective life if conception is not, in the end, a viable option, or does not happen. But of course counselling addresses very many other issues. In fact, there's hardly an issue which can't be clarified by the right kind of counselling.

Some Case Histories

The following case histories are of ordinary people who, at a serious crossroads in their lives, have decided to seek professional help. In some cases, they sought counselling of their own accord; in others, they were referred by their doctors or other professionals. Their experiences should give you an idea of the variety of problems which appropriate counselling can address.

Annette

For many years Annette had been secretly unhappy with her marriage. Her own parents had divorced when she was young and she did not want to repeat that pattern, to feel that she could not make a success of her personal relationships. But there was no longer any real communication between Annette and her husband Bill; all they seemed to do was have endless rows.

After twenty years of marriage, things came to a head when a so-called 'holiday of a lifetime' turned into a fortnight of bitter rows and recriminations. For the first time, Annette wondered seriously about a divorce. She was nervous – she had not been in paid employment since she was married, after which Bill's job had taken them all over the world, and although the house was in joint names, she had no idea how to set about earning a living again.

She wondered whether marriage guidance could help at all and decided to broach the subject with Bill. He was extremely resistant, saying that he did not want outsiders and do-gooders interfering in his life, though when Annette told him she couldn't go on any more as they were, he reluctantly agreed to see a marriage guidance counsellor.

Bill, however, either didn't turn up at all for the sessions or turned up late, and when he did turn up he was hostile all the way through. He took an instant dislike to the counsellor and after the first few sessions said he would not go any more. It all seemed to be a dismal failure. But although the counselling sessions did not seem to be getting anywhere as far as patching up the relationship was concerned, they helped Annette face a fundamental truth – that she and Bill no longer had anything in common, they could not communicate, and there was no real future in a life together.

She says: 'It was during those counselling sessions that I came to realize just how far apart Bill and I had become. We simply did not see life in the same way, and there was no possibility of making the relationship work unless I was prepared to make compromises I was no longer prepared to make.

'Going for counselling helped to give me the courage to divorce Bill, and live apart. He was extremely reluctant, and felt things could go on as they were, pretending, but I was getting desperate.'

Since going for initial counselling, and her divorce, Annette has discovered that she is far more prepared to look at herself and her reasons for wanting to stay in the marriage, for wanting to get out, for wanting some kind of security.

'After the marriage guidance counselling, I joined a women's group and then booked up some sessions with a feminist counsellor,' she said. 'It's been painful at times, but I feel I'm no longer sweeping things under the carpet and trying to make the best of everything. I'm becoming, for the first time in my life, my own person.

'But I had to be ready to go for counselling. Bill wasn't –

and he still isn't, with the result that, four years after our divorce, he still believes that one day I'll come back to him.'

Gloria

Gloria's world fell apart when her only child, Imogen, suddenly died at the age of five. Always a healthy, lively child, Imogen was dead within a week of being struck down by a devastating illness. Gloria, a high-flying career woman, had been over forty when Imogen was born and there was virtually no chance she would ever be able to have another child. She was also a single parent; had never wanted to be married.

Life suddenly seemed to have no meaning. Gloria had always prided herself on her strength and her ability to cope with every situation, and had been scornful of counsellors, so when the social worker who visited her after the sudden death suggested a bereavement counsellor, Gloria could not face the idea. The social worker persuaded her to give the counsellor a try, and Gloria reluctantly agreed.

Now, a year after Imogen's death, she says: 'I'm not saying that the counsellor helped me to get over it, but she certainly helped me to come to terms with my loss, and to put it into perspective.

'She didn't say any ridiculous things about other people being worse off than I was, or that time would be a great healer. But she did explain how bereaved people go through a series of emotions, and that each one is to be expected.

'Her input also helped me to cope with the funeral, so that in an odd kind of way I quite enjoyed it. Hundreds of people turned up, as they will for the sudden death of a small child, and, with a friend, I planned it so that there was a proper service and no denial of the fact that Imogen had died.

'The counsellor also advised me to keep talking about it, not to try and deny or pretend that it hadn't happened, or to blame doctors, nurses or teachers for her death. That, she said, is all part of the denial of reality, and can delay healing and the ability to live one's life again.'

Gloria discovered, to her surprise, that the issue of bereavement was far more complicated than just going through a period of grieving. 'Through the counselling, I came to know myself so much better than before, and it certainly helped me to accept the reality of Imogen's death, even though it did not really touch the actual grief.

'Above all, I think, my counsellor gave me permission to grieve openly, not to try to bottle it up; to talk about it, and also to know who my real friends were – not always the people I imagined would be supportive.'

Joy

The experience of sudden, unexpected death will often be what brings people into counselling. Joy had been living with Mike for ten years and they had just decided, after years working for other people, to start up in business together. Then Mike was suddenly killed in a car crash, at the age of forty-three.

Joy, numbed by the shock, felt that somehow she had to be able to speak to Mike. That seemed the most important thing – there was so much she had wanted to say to him. A friend suggested seeing a psychic counsellor and although Joy did not believe in such things, her grief was so great, so uncontainable, she agreed at least to try it.

Joy said: 'A friend recommended a psychic counsellor who she said was completely above board and reliable. I was extremely sceptical, but I went. The counsellor first enabled me to accept the reality of death and also talked about death being by no means the end. I don't know whether I believe this, but it was certainly comforting at the time.

'We talked about how I viewed death, she told me how spiritualists view death, and I said that, above all, I wanted to be able to contact him, to talk to him. The counsellor, who was also a medium, did get in touch with him, or appeared to, and I spoke to him through her. It certainly seemed to be Mike, although of course I could not be completely sure.

'But I felt so much better after contacting him, as if I had finished the unfinished business between us. He told me to go ahead and start the business anyway, which, after a few months, I found the strength to do.'

It is eight months since Mike died and Joy is functioning. She is coping, although sometimes the loneliness is terrible and she longs only to be with him. But she has, on her own, set up the photocopying business she and Mike intended to start together, and feels at peace since she spoke to him after his death.

'I had no religious faith,' she said, 'so a vicar or priest wouldn't have been the right people to talk to. I suddenly felt drawn to see the psychic counsellor – and now I don't know how I would have managed if I hadn't been able to communicate with Mike. I don't know whether I'll ever get over him, or find anybody else – at the moment this seems unlikely – but the counselling helped me over a patch when I couldn't cope at all on my own.'

Paul

Paul, at the age of thirty-one, was made redundant at work. It was a situation beyond his control: around five hundred jobs were to be lost from the engineering company where he had worked for the past seven years. As part of its policy, the company had redundancy counsellors available for anybody who wanted to talk to them.

Paul said: 'At first I thought it was patronizing and artificial to have these redundancy counsellors available. All I wanted was to keep my job. I'd recently got married and we had bought a house with a huge mortgage. Now, I had no idea how we were going to keep up the payments.

'But then I thought, hell, I've got nothing to lose, and fixed up a session with the counsellor. It was free, so I wasn't going to have to add insult to injury by paying for it.

'The counsellor was a man in his forties who had been made redundant twice and had decided to train as a counsellor to help others cope with this modern problem. I told him at the outset that if he wasn't able to get me another job right away, I wasn't prepared to listen to him.

'He told me he couldn't possibly get me another job but would help me to come to terms with this sudden loss. We talked through my feelings about being made redundant and the counsellor explained that the way I coped with this redundancy would help to shape my attitude when I went for job interviews.

'I was surprised at how much rage and resentment I felt at my firm for sacking me. We also uncovered strong feelings of inadequacy – after all, although five hundred jobs were to be lost, lots of my colleagues had kept theirs. And with me, it wasn't even as if it was a case of last in, first out, since I had been there seven years.

'I also discovered a perfectionist streak in myself and difficulty in delegating. But thanks to the counselling, I didn't feel bitter, rejected and on the scrap heap. The sessions – we had three in all – helped me to have a positive attitude towards applying for jobs. I was also helped to see that rage and resentment, although natural, were not helpful and that my employers didn't personally dislike me.

'I started applying for jobs right away after the counselling, used my redundancy money to pay off a chunk of the mortgage and, after five rejections, got another job in a similar kind of firm. The job's not so well paid as my other one, but at least I'm in work.

'I now think that the counselling helped me to get over the pain of being made redundant, and wondering what was wrong with me. It also helped to give me the confidence to prepare a new CV and apply for jobs with confidence.'

Malcolm

At the age of twenty-nine, Malcolm was diagnosed HIV positive. He had been in a gay relationship with his boyfriend for about seven years and assumed that Alan was as faithful as he had been himself. But, obviously not. Alan had been Malcolm's first and only partner, so he was particularly devastated by the diagnosis. As part of his treatment, Malcolm was offered counselling – and found there was a bewildering variety of counselling available for those diagnosed HIV positive.

'I didn't know at first what would be right for me, and I tried a number of different organizations,' he said. 'Eventually, I came across a charity which offered telephone help plus face to face counselling whenever it was needed – and it's helped me to deal with all the feelings of pain, rage, hatred, the homophobia of our present society, and how to deal with any new relationships.

'It was very hard for me to forgive Alan but through the counselling I was helped to see that bearing grudges and resentments was only going to make the illness worse, by adding to the burden of stress on my body.

'So far, I've been perfectly well and don't know when, or if, I shall develop full-blown AIDS. The counselling service has helped me to understand the positions regarding insurance, jobs, telling other people, coping with it myself.

'When something like HIV strikes, you find you have no coping skills at all – at least, I hadn't. I had no idea how to live with it, work through it, come to terms with it.'

Margaret

Margaret had been on tranquillizers for fifteen years and desperately wanted to come off them, though she didn't know how she would ever be able to do so and felt she needed some kind of expert help. Her doctor recommended a specialist tranquillizer counsellor, who, he said, had successfully withdrawn from tranquillizers herself and would be able to help. The counsellor, who is in private practice, told Margaret exactly what to expect and how to work through it.

'Even with the counsellor's help, withdrawing wasn't easy,' Margaret said. 'I found I had to cope not only with the physical withdrawal symptoms but also with the underlying emotional problem which had led to me taking tranquillizers in the first place. It was still there, even after all these years, and underneath the tranquillizer effect, had been actually getting stronger. So now, instead of one problem, I had two – coping with withdrawal and with my own emotions.

'I went through rage, hatred, hostility of the doctors who had prescribed such drugs in the first place, the drug company for manufacturing them and conning us all, myself for being fool enough to take them. I also railed at the people who had caused my emotional problem in the first place.

'I wondered how on earth it would be possible to get through life without tranquillizers. My children and my partner had never known me untranquillized. I didn't know what sort of person I was either, and I was frightened.

'I'm not saying that my many sessions of tranquillizer counselling made it easy for me to come off them but it certainly made it possible. I also got to know myself better through counselling and realized I wasn't such a weak and fearful person as I had imagined. I like myself better now, undrugged, and counselling helped me to find the real me inside all the fears, addictions and the fog which had descended through the tranquillized years.'

Edward

Edward was not happy at university. He felt he was reading the wrong subject, Geography, and he did not seem able to make friends easily. Also, he was a long way from home. He mentioned his fears about reading the wrong subject to his personal tutor, who suggested that he saw the student counsellor, who was there to help with just this problem.

Edward said: 'The student counsellor saved my life. I can't really speak too highly of him. He was tremendously experienced, and the service was free, as well. It emerged that I was reading the wrong subject and the counsellor helped me to change to anthropology, which suits me far better.

'We also discussed the problem of not being able to make friends and my homesickness. It took me quite a long time to work through this and to realize the reasons for it, which were far more deep-seated than I had imagined and had to do with my relationship with my mother. She never wanted to let me go, and hated the idea that I was grown up and able to live away from home. But I learned not to blame her and to realize that it was up to me to grow up.

'I still find it quite hard to make friends, as I am basically very shy, but clarifying the position has made me feel a lot happier about myself generally. I'm certainly glad that the student counselling service existed – I wouldn't have known what to do otherwise, as I had nobody at all to talk to.'

Robert

Robert, at the age of thirty-three, was badly injured when the train he was travelling on crashed into another. For months he was off work and even after he had recovered physically, he found it difficult to get back into the swing of things. He was a chartered accountant with a young family, and he kept suffering periods of black depression. He would think he had put the whole event behind him, and then it would return to haunt him again. Eventually, after several years, his depression became so bad that he went to see his doctor. Instead of pre-scribing anti-depressants, Robert's doctor, who knew about the train crash, suggested that he might like to see a trauma counsellor.

'A what?' Robert asked, having no idea such people existed. 'But that train crash was years ago; surely I should have got over it by now?'

'I don't know much about it,' the doctor admitted, 'but if you like, I can refer you.'

'Well, all right,' Robert said.

The trauma counsellor started by asking Robert to write down his dreams and then helped him to have happier memories of the incident by suggesting different endings to the crash. The counsellor realized that Robert was suffering from post-traumatic stress disorder, which commonly results in extreme anxiety, nightmares and intrusive memories, and the method of counselling he used has been successful for victims of many major air and train crashes.

Since the incident, Robert had not dared travel on a train, so he drove into work, which put a couple of hours onto his working day. With his counsellor's help, he gradually became able to stand on a station platform, then to board a train and get off, and eventually to make a short journey.

He said: 'I didn't think I'd ever be able to travel on a train again. But now I am using the train to get to work and although I occasionally still have panic attacks, I'm coping.'

The examples just given are very simplified accounts of what happened during counselling. They are not meant to give the impression that counselling has a guaranteed positive outcome, or that it is all plain sailing. Not every problem, by any means, is immediately amenable to counselling, nor can counselling solve every single problem. Some people do not get better, some may attempt or succeed in suicide, or sometimes the counselling does not seem to touch them.

Counselling cannot be guaranteed to help, it is not foolproof or without complications, drawbacks and difficulties of its own. But professional counsellors, to whom your problem, whatever it might be, is not new, can often help people to face up to their own problems, to improve their attitude, to replace negative with positive thinking, and feel better about themselves. Anybody who is in any kind of trouble can, theoretically at least, benefit from counselling, and nobody should imagine that they cannot ever be helped by it. But sometimes it takes courage, or a crisis, to admit to yourself that you may need help.

Are You Ready for Counselling?

Nobody can dragoon you into going for counselling. If you do not feel ready for it, or do not believe that a counsellor can help you, then it may be better not to go. Great resistance is always counter-productive, as with Bill, Annette's husband. He did not see the point of counselling, he still does not see the point of it, and has decided, for the time being, not to grow, not to face up to the reality of himself.

For everybody, the time has to be right. Clearly, some situations, such as sudden death or serious illness, will catapult people into seeking counselling when they might not otherwise have done so. People suffering from serious, presently incurable illnesses such as AIDS and certain forms of cancer will almost certainly be able to see a counsellor.

But what about more amorphous situations, where you can't exactly put your finger on a problem but can't quite ever seem to get things to work for you? Perhaps you can't understand why you're not getting promotion at work, when people more junior and with less experience are promoted above your head; perhaps you can't manage your money, or live on your income; perhaps you dread going to see your parents, but don't really know why;

perhaps you are plagued by anxiety and stress every time you are asked to make a speech in public.

Counselling may well be appropriate for all these situations but before placing all your hopes in it as the solution, it is important to be clear about what it can offer. Counselling can't, for instance, magically mend a crumbling marriage. It can't bring back prosperity or alter your bank balance – except perhaps to make it lower, as you will very probably have to pay the counsellor – and it can't put a family back together again.

Counselling cannot make somebody love you. It cannot alter somebody else's behaviour. It cannot make your spouse or partner change. The only person counselling can ever change is you – so long as you are prepared to accept the possibility of change in your life. Basically, counselling enables you to take responsibility for your actions, personality and lifestyle.

Consider the case of Arthur. A brilliant pupil, he gained ten A grades at O level when just fifteen. At sixteen, he won a scholarship to Oxford. At seventeen, with three good A levels behind him, he embarked on a year out to America, where he had a wonderful time. Then he went up to Oxford to read philosophy, and found that there were other students just as brilliant as he was. He did very little work and ended up with a mediocre degree.

He had no idea what to do when he left university and took a series of odd jobs. In the end, in desperation, he qualified as a cost and works accountant. He got a job with the local gas board and married a secretary there. After five years and with one child, the marriage broke up.

Pauline, his wife, got everything – or, at least, that's how Arthur saw it. He left his job at the gas board and enrolled as a mature student at art college. After graduating, he tried to make a living as an artist but found this was impossible. He taught art for a couple of years and then remarried. This marriage lasted less than a year, although this time there were no children. Now, at forty, Arthur is on the dole, wondering whatever happened to his potential, his intelligence, the wonderful success he was going to make of his life.

Arthur has never been for counselling but at this stage in his life he might do well to consider it. The right kind of counsellor would help him to understand why things have never gone right, what childhood or parental influences might have contributed to his perceived lack of personal fulfilment, and help him to get himself back into some kind of functional lifestyle.

What a counsellor cannot do is get Arthur a job, give him more money or get the half-share he believes he deserves in his former house. Effective counselling would help Arthur to see the patterns that have shaped his life so far.

Now consider Arlette. At school, Arlette was considered a very gifted actress. She got into RADA and soon fell in love with a fellow student. They married when Arlette was nineteen and had two children. It seemed impossible for Arlette to continue with her acting, so she gave up her career while Trevor, her husband, tried to support them by his acting.

For a time, they were miserably poor. Then Trevor landed a small part in a television sitcom. That small part led to bigger parts and Trevor soon became a household name. Arlette, meanwhile, had never worked as an actress since graduating. Trevor fell in love with one of his leading ladies, a glamorous young rising actress, and left Arlette.

Now, aged thirty-five and with two children aged twelve and ten, Arlette believes that life has passed her by. She feels she is losing her looks, she has no profession and cannot keep herself as she gets older. She is now an unhappy housewife and mother: how did it all happen, and what can she do to get herself out of this miserable situation?

Like Arthur, Arlette could benefit from counselling. Again, she would be enabled to see the patterns in her life, the reasons for her disappointment, and be helped to gain strategies for making her life more effective in future. Through counselling, both Arthur and Arlette would be able to get to know themselves, not to blame others, and to take responsibility for themselves – the main outcome of successful counselling.

Who Counselling Can Help

Very few of us have the strength to cope entirely on our own. Also, when considering something new or possibly irreversible, such as cosmetic surgery, actual information is needed, so that the risks and benefits can be measured and assessed. It is helpful, perhaps, to think of counsellors as experts in their field, like lawyers, plumbers or doctors. When you need professional help, you go to a professional. Think of counsellors as people who are there to serve you, not to persuade you or to give specific advice, but to clarify issues, to help you to see difficulties in ways you perhaps had not considered before, and to bring out the best in you.

The following list is by no means comprehensive but it should give you a picture of the variety of problems with which counselling deals and who can be helped by counselling:

Those who are stuck in a relationship which seems to be going nowhere;
Those for whom personal relationships never seem to be satisfying;
Those who would like to be more effective generally;
Those who can't seem to recover from a past emotional hurt;
Those suffering from serious illness;
People who have been abused or mistreated as children;
Women who feel overwhelmed and insignificant in a patriarchal society;
Those wanting to come off drugs or addictive medication;

People who would like to have a more positive attitude to life;

Anybody who has been bereaved;

Anybody who has witnessed or been caught up in a traumatic event, such as a serious car or plane crash;

Anybody who has suffered a reversal of fortune, such as physical disability, loss of job, or home property;

Those who are suffering stress at work or home;

People who feel they just can't cope, and don't know why;

Those who seem to go from one bad relationship to another;

Those who believe they may be gay, or have other sexual difficulties;

People who feel lonely;

Anybody who has loved and lost somebody dear;

Anybody considering drastic physical changes to themselves, such as cosmetic surgery, sterilization or a sex-change operation;

Anybody interested in 'personal growth'.

3

How Counselling Works

One of the questions many people have about counselling is: what actually goes on in the counselling room? Both the practicalities and the process itself may seem shrouded in mystery and hence give rise to all sorts of misapprehensions and fears. Although nobody can tell you exactly what will happen in counselling, simply because every client (and every counsellor) is different, it can certainly help to know generally what to expect – and what you should *not* expect. This chapter therefore aims to give you a general picture of how counselling works, of what goes on between counsellor and client, both to allay doubts and fears about it, and to enable you as a client to know whether the counselling is being carried out professionally.

The Counselling Contract

Counselling involves an agreement, albeit unwritten, between you and the counsellor, and though the terms may vary there are certain basic points to it.

The first is that confidentiality is essential. Counselling should provide a safe space where people can release their innermost feelings, their prejudices, their pent-up anger, their problems, without feeling they are losing face, exposing themselves or being judged harshly. Within the counselling relationship, any old rubbish can come out and the counsellor will (or should) listen attentively, without disapproval and with understanding. What is said is between you and the counsellor, not for public consumption. Counsellors should never tell your doctor, your employer, your partner, what has been divulged during counselling – not, at least, without your permission.

This confidentiality, a cornerstone of counselling, does not exclude the counsellor from talking about you, again in confidence, to her or his supervisor – who is, or should be, someone with considerable counselling experience. You may be concerned about the idea of being discussed in supervision, and indeed it demands you having trust in the counsellor, but it is important to see it as a safeguard for you rather than as a threat. Supervision is there to help counsellors by clarifying where they are in the counselling with you, to provide guidelines and support for them. In fact, you should be much more concerned if your counsellor does not have any supervision, as this is one of the prerequisites of professional practice.

Providing a safe space also means, on a practical level, meeting in a room that is private and quiet, where you are not disturbed by anyone else walking in or distracted by telephone calls or loud noise. You should expect, always, to meet in this same room. Having said that, counsellors cannot always be expected to provide the ideal conditions and if you go for counselling in, say, a busy counselling centre, you may have to accept occasional shifting around or background noise.

You will probably be asked to come for an initial interview (sometimes called an intake or assessment), which, if it is in a counselling centre rather than with a counsellor in private practice, will not usually be with the counsellor you eventually see. (Some counselling organizations may require you to fill in a form beforehand, giving some details about yourself and your reasons for seeking help.)

The initial interview, for which you may be expected to pay, is to talk over your problem generally and agree on your counselling goal – though the goal or goals may change in nature during the counselling. You will also be asked questions about your age, background, present circumstances, family and medical history. Do not be surprised if in talking about yourself, you become very emotional, and do not hesitate to ask questions yourself about the counsellor's qualifications and way of working. If you are going for private counselling, you may want to see more than one counsellor before making your choice – though bear in mind that counsellors are also free to say whether they are willing to take you on and aren't necessarily going to be able to keep spaces vacant for long.

At the initial interview, or with the counsellor to whom you are later assigned, you will agree terms about money, time and other practicalities. Some counselling services are provided free, for example, the student and redudancy counselling described in the previous chapter which helped Paul and Edward; other organizations will ask you for a fee or a voluntary contribution according to your financial circumstances, while counsellors in private practice will have their own charges – these are discussed further in Chapter 7.

Counselling time is usually on the basis of one session a week lasting fifty minutes – the so-called therapeutic hour – though sessions, particularly for group, marital and family counselling, may last longer or be less frequent than once a week. The overall period of time on which you agree that the counselling will go on can vary greatly. It is very rare for a single session to be enough to resolve an issue, though this does sometimes happen. Mostly, counselling falls into short-term and long-term agreements. A common short-term agreement would be for six or twelve sessions, maybe with a review at the end of that time to consider whether to continue – and if so, this may be agreed for a further specified number of sessions.

In longer-term counselling, the agreement might be for

an outside limit of one year, or two years, possibly with reviews at agreed intermediate stages, and with the understanding that the limit is a maximum not a minimum – you may well not need as long as this (or there may be circumstances where it is agreed to extend the maximum). As a general rule, counsellors in private practice are able to give more flexibility and usually offer long-term rather than short-term counselling, without rigid limits. Many counselling services are now under increasing demand, at a time of financial and social service cut-backs, and may have to impose limits to try to cope.

Counselling, however, should not anyway be seen as open-ended, a place where you can continue *ad infinitum* to pour out your problems. All counselling is goal-oriented, whether it is about acquiring 'life skills' or to learn to cope with a specific problem, such as bereavement, marital breakdown or redundancy. It is not just an opportunity for you to air your grievances and have a shoulder to cry on, but a journey of self-exploration with the aim of helping you gain independence and autonomy, without relying on the counsellor to give you the strength you feel you lack yourself. Don't imagine that counsellors will always know what the outcome will be. The journey is often as interesting and uncharted for them as it is for you.

Although all counsellors have their own methods, and are trained to be flexible, counselling work usually follows a pattern of a beginning, middle and end phase, and there will sometimes be specific goals which the counsellor will hope to reach with you during these phases. What to expect during these phases is described later in the chapter.

The Counsellor's Skills

All good counsellors should have two particular skills at their fingertips – listening ability and empathy. In fact, these are the most important attributes of any counsellor and the reasons why counselling can work so well. As these are so very important, we will look a little more closely at what exactly they are.

The ability to listen, really listen, is much rarer than you might imagine. It is not a question of just hearing what is being said but an active, creative act in which the counsellor concentrates entirely on you as the client. This quality of listening is not necessarily an innate gift but something which can be learnt – and which is an essential part of every counsellor's training. It is a demanding skill which requires confidence and self-assurance on the part of the listener.

Good listening assumes that the speaker has dignity and value and is saying something important. It is not the job of a counsellor to be liked and counsellors will not (or should not) worry about what impression they are making on you. They should be giving a hundred per cent to you and in doing so are offering you unconditional love and regard, even if you are describing horrific events and negative feelings connected with your past or present.

Good listeners – and all professional counsellors are good listeners, or they ought to be in another job – are processing information as they hear it and storing it away. They should remember what you have told them. They will also make eye contact and have their minds and bodies 'tuned in' to you. This means that counsellors should sit in an attentive posture and not fiddle with hair, nails or items of dress. They may prompt you with phrases such as 'Go on' or draw you out by asking you to clarify or expand on specific points.

One way that counsellors show they are listening is to repeat back to you what you have just said. For example, if you say: 'I had a really lousy childhood', your counsellor may say: 'You had a lousy childhood. In what way was it lousy?'

Good listeners are able not just to tune into what is being said but to note your feelings and body language as you are speaking. They will not necessarily comment on this, but will use their appraisal to try to gain a clear picture of why you have come, what you are hoping to gain from counselling and what, if any, are the differences between what you are saying and what you actually mean and feel.

In order to be a good listener, the counsellor has to concentrate wholly on you, and not be distracted, in order both to hear what you are saying and evaluate and respond to your words as well. Since all counsellors are fallible humans, they won't always be the totally perfect listener, but if your counsellor is a good listener, you will be able to sense this straightaway – there will be an almost palpable atmosphere of listening in the room.

Counsellors are, above all, people who set out especially to listen to you – usually when nobody else will, or when nobody else seems to understand. Although we all believe we are good listeners, creative listening is actually quite rare and many people new to counselling are astonished to find that this is the first time that anybody has ever really listened to them. One reason that counselling is becoming ever more popular is that in a busy, noisy world, here are people whose actual job it is to listen to you.

The second counselling skill, empathy, is, if possible, even more important than listening ability. The American therapist Carl Rogers, who in many ways can be considered the father of present-day counselling, and who developed a type of non-authoritarian counselling known as 'client-centred', defined empathy as the ability to enter another person's world, the ability to sense meanings both at and below the surface, and in doing so help clients to experience themselves more fully and move forward to take responsibility for their own actions.

There is always an emotional climate of respect and acceptance when there is empathy. This allows clients to feel safe and free to reveal themselves as they are, without the defensive barriers which they may have erected over the years. Counsellors who possess empathy will not try to impose their own wishes and attitudes, but will accept where you are in life. Empathy is not, however, the same as sympathy – the counsellor will not necessarily condone actions, or allow self-pity to continue, but she or he will try to understand just how you became capable of performing certain actions, or how it was possible to experience a particular range of feelings.

Empathy means that the counsellor understands your feelings, but remains detached from their direct experience for you. Where there is sympathy (by contrast), a counsellor may attempt actually to experience the same feelings as the client and become so personally affected that the client feels suffocated. But empathy is different – it means that the counsellor does not experience these feelings directly, but knows what you are going through and allows you to express it.

You, as the client, will soon know whether your counsellor has empathy or not. If she or he does not, you will have the feeling you are never getting through, that you cannot make yourself clear.

The Beginning Phase

This is when you establish a rapport with your counsellor, get to know her or him and work out the reasons why you have come for counselling. In the first session you should discuss how long the counselling is expected to last, how much it is going to cost, and when and for how long the sessions will be .

Arrive on time. The session won't be extended because you're late, or only in rare circumstances, and lateness will probably be understood as a form of self-sabotage stemming from lack of self-respect; it punishes you, not the counsellor. It may sound obvious, but if you know it is unavoidable that you are going to be very late, telephone in advance to warn the counsellor.

Counsellors know that they are often regarded rather like dentists – with a mixture of fear and dread – and that it often takes a lot of courage to book up counselling sessions, so congratulate yourself when you finally make it. You will probably feel slightly tense and nervous at first, which again counsellors realize and they should be able to put you at your ease right away. It helps of course if you are going in a willing spirit, not reluctantly or under sufferance. The more positive you are, the more eager to have a positive outcome, the greater is likely to be the benefit.

In the beginning phase, the counsellor will be asking questions to find out why you have come, and why you are experiencing the feelings you are at present. A good counsellor will never try to deny the reality of your feelings. If you say: 'I always felt so unattractive as a child, that I was stupid and clumsy', the counsellor will say something like: 'Why exactly did you feel so stupid and clumsy?' She or he will *not* say: 'That's nonsense. How could you feel stupid and clumsy?'

With each question, the counsellor will be trying to draw you out, trying to encourage you to define your terms, to express exactly how you see your problem. The counsellor's task is to listen attentively to you, to any rantings and ravings, any blame or recriminations, against other people or yourself. She or he will be trying to understand, not argue with you or attempt to make you change your feelings. You may be saturated with gentle but insistent questions to make it more clear about how you feel and what you want from counselling.

Don't worry if you do not seem able to express yourself very well, or you can't remember incidents from the past. Few of us are used to talking about our personal feelings and also it is in the nature of painful incidents that they are buried in order for us to survive them – but they never really go away until we can face them, bring them to the surface and release them. The counsellor should understand all this and try to help you express why you have decided to seek help.

She or he will be trying to get a picture of you from what you don't say with words, as well as what you actually say, for your body language may indicate unspoken anxieties. For example, fidgeting, folded arms, legs twisted round each other, hand-to-face gestures, may all speak volumes about your emotions, about whether you are open and expansive, or defensive and guarded.

But counsellors are not gods and they may get it wrong, misinterpret or not understand some of the things you are trying to tell them. Good counsellors will rarely, at this stage, interpret what you say but will ask you to elaborate on statements you have made. They may just seem to repeat things back to you, rather than taking the conversation any further. For instance, if you say: 'I've been worried about my work lately,' the response may be: 'You've been worried about your work. Would you like to elaborate on that a bit?'

The idea is to draw you out, to try to find out just what the problems are, both those you are talking about and those you may be hiding. For at the heart of all counselling is the understanding that presenting problems are not always the same as the underlying ones. For instance, your problem may be a persistent skin complaint that is making your life a misery but it may come clear in counselling that the complaint always erupts when you are repressing some deeply felt rage – and it is the underlying anger with which you really need help.

It is the job of the counsellor to help you to see and accept the underlying reasons for problems in the present. Counsellors do not give you answers on a plate – indeed, they don't have them – but they will help you to see things for yourself, so that you realize why things have happened as they have, and can then decide on your own answer.

Counsellor Jenny Bateman, who trains potential counsellors as well as counselling personnel in industry and individually, says: 'My job is basically to help people sort out what they want. When a new client comes to me, I have to try and decide whether the presenting problem is the actual one, or whether there is something deeper and more disturbing behind it all. Very often, somebody may come to me complaining of stress at work, for instance, and through talking, we start to discover that there are many other deeper-rooted problems, that the stress at work is only a symptom.

'Frequently we find that talking about one issue triggers off thoughts and memories about something else, which may have been hidden for many years.

'Most of us put up barriers which separate us from other people. If we have been hurt in our early years, there is a tendency to become stuck and repeat unhelpful patterns. Also, when people have not addressed their problems, or taken responsibility for their actions, they become stuck in destructive patterns which surface as stress, as something which has a name.

'I'm very aware that my clients look to me for answers,' Jenny said. 'I have to tell them at the outset that I haven't got all the answers, that we have to try and work through the problems together.'

If, for instance, you go into counselling complaining about being under stress at work, your counsellor might ask how long the stress has been going on, when you first became aware of it, whether there are any particular times when you notice the stress is especially bad; whether you suffered stress in all your jobs or just this one; whether you suffered stress as a child, and so on. Through asking such questions, the counsellor (and gradually you yourself in thinking about the answers) will be building up a composite picture of your stress, your attitude to it, your way of dealing with it, and the reasons why you cannot seem to get on top of it.

At this beginning stage, most clients tend to think their counsellors are absolutely wonderful: founts of all wisdom, impossibly good, serene, untroubled, clear thinking, super-human beings. But as you move into the middle phase of counselling, your feelings may well undergo a dramatic change.

The Middle Phase

This is where both counsellor and client get down to the nitty gritty, as you explore your feelings further. At this stage, the counsellor may well suggest some interpretations of what is going on. She or he may suggest, for instance, that your stress at work is connected with feelings of failure and rejection, or having an impossible ideal of perfectionism. Perhaps it will be suggested that you tend to seek approval, that you want to be loved, that you want people to believe you are a coper, somebody who never gets upset or nervous. It may be suggested that you believe you can't really do the job, that you fear you may be found out and given the sack.

Counsellors are not (or should not be) trying to put thoughts into your head but are asking you to examine your attitudes a little more closely, so that pieces of the jigsaw fall into place. If the counselling is working, you should feel clarification during the middle phase. If you don't – then the counselling is not working for you and you need to ask yourself if this is because of your own attitude or the counsellor's. Either way, bring up your doubts in the session. All the time you are talking, counsellors will be asking themselves questions about you, such as: why is this person in this particular state at the moment? They will be suggesting answers, but don't forget that you are on a journey of exploration together. The counsellor doesn't necessarily *know* the answers.

One important question is to ask what changes in your life are realistically possible. For instance, you may reveal that you've always harboured a secret desire to be a ballerina and may blame your parents for never letting you have ballet lessons as a child. This dream is most unlikely to be alizable, but if it has always been with you, it won't necessarily go away just because you know logically that it is now too late to do anything about it.

Hearing about your lifelong dream, your counsellor may suggest that you find work with a ballet company, in some administrative or other behind-the-scenes position, or that you might like to learn some kind of dancing which you can perform at any age, such as tap or circle dancing. Gradually, by asking questions and getting you to clarify your position, your counsellor will enable you to discover whether this dream of being a dancer was ever a serious one, and whether you genuinely want to be in the ballet world. It could be that underneath you are not – but you have kept this dream going to avoid facing up to what your potential might be. Through blaming others for your lack of chances, it may be that you have never really taken responsibility for your own life.

Similarly, you may always have had a secret dream about being a writer, but your father made you train as a chartered accountant and enter the family firm. During this middle phase of counselling, your counsellor will try to help you discover why you never did become a writer, why you never sent off short stories, enrolled for a writing course, or defied your father and refused to train as an accountant.

Your counsellor will give you the opportunity to discover why you never seemed to gain what you wanted (or thought you wanted) from life. Counsellors do not suggest motivations and actions in the way that a barrister in court might. Their queryings are aimed at enabling you to see for yourself what led you to certain kinds of action in the past.

At this stage, childhood difficulties may crop up. If it seems relevant, your counsellor will ask you questions about your home life, your family, your background – again, not with the intention of judging this, but to try to help you put it all into perspective, to understand the reality rather than the fantasy.

Often, clients find that everything swings along in the beginning phase of counselling, only for them to get bogged down in the middle phase. Here, you should be prepared for counselling to become painful and slow, with progress uneven. When this happens, it is probably because the counsellor – and you – are touching on difficult issues, things you find difficult to talk about or bring into the open. Experienced counsellors will be prepared for sticky patches and should be able to guide you through them.

Also, as the sessions proceed, you may start thinking your counsellor is not so brilliant after all. They may not even seem to be on your side. They may suggest things to you that you don't like, and the early positive feelings may be replaced by ones of dislike or discomfort. This is perfectly normal, if unpleasant. The counsellor should be used to it and should be able to deal with your hostile, uncomfortable feelings.

There may be tears, a feeling of catharsis, a feeling of hopelessness. Emotions may swing wildly between one session and the next. You may leave the session feeling happy and positive, and then during the week – or before the next session – something happens to dampen your mood. So expect starts and stops, periods of resistance, fury, rage. All these emotions are well known to counsellors and they will be looking out for them.

During the middle phase of counselling, if progress is to be made, there has to be acknowledgement from you as the client that the problem – whatever it is – is yours and will not go away until you change your attitude or behaviour. Sometimes there may be nothing you can do to alter the problem itself – somebody suffering from terminal cancer, for instance, may have to accept that a cure is not possible – but counselling works from the belief that, however intractable the problem, a positive acceptance and understanding of the position can help.

Blame, either of yourself or other people in your life, is

not encouraged. Instead, the aim is to help clients come to an understanding that blame – all the 'shoulds' and 'if onlys' – are ways in which we seek to evade responsibility for our actions. Feelings of bitterness and resentment may be inevitable but blame is ultimately considered negative and unhelpful.

Although you may gain great insights during counselling sessions, do not imagine it will be easy to change your behaviour or attitudes. Old habits, as they say, die hard and it may take a long time to replace an old, negative outlook with a new positive one. There are likely to be many ups and downs on the way and sessions may be highly emotional.

Counsellors should never minimize your feelings or try to discount what you may see as a serious trauma in your life. If you say: 'My mother promised to take me to the zoo and she never did,' a good counsellor will *not* reply: 'Lots of mothers make promises they never fulfil – that's nothing.' Instead, the response will be to ask you to explain more fully why you should have been so upset by this broken promise, why the memory of it has stayed in your mind for so many years.

It's important to realize that effective counselling goes through peaks and troughs, and that people rarely get better, become healed, on a smooth upward scale. A feeling of progress is often followed by a definite downturn. There may well be times when the client feels stuck and as if there is no workable solution to the many problems. But experienced counsellors are used to this and will have faith in the counselling process.

For instance, you may have come to counselling with serious marriage difficulties. While you may believe that the relationship is at an end, you may at the same time be putting up many objections to leaving the situation.

A woman may say: 'I'd like to leave him, but what would I live on? Where would I go? What if I don't get the children? What if he won't pay maintenance? How will I get a job and support myself after not having worked for twenty years?'

The counsellor's job is to try to get you to clarify the reasons for your objections and to enable you to understand that there are always choices but that every choice involves a price. Only you can decide which price is too high.

During counselling, you may decide that life is so intolerable with your spouse that you want to get out however cold and forbidding the outside world seems. Or, it may be that your fears of managing on your own are so great that, for you, the price is just too high to pay. You would, deep down, rather have the security that being in a relationship brings, even though the relationship is not good.

In the latter case, the counsellor will try to help you to see how the relationship can be improved; how you can change your attitude, become more positively assertive, less complaining, more autonomous, without disrupting the whole family. The counsellor will also help you to see that you can never ever change anybody else, that the only person you can ever hope to change is yourself – and that's hard enough work.

If you have gone for counselling because of a devastating change in your life such as the death of someone close to you, or a serious illness or accident, the main task of the counsellor at this stage will be to get you gradually to accept the reality of what has happened, not to try to deny it, nor the mix of feelings aroused in you. It happened, and it won't unhappen. Acceptance, though, can be extremely difficult and good counsellors will be patient as you work your way through your feelings. They won't try to rush you but will proceed at your pace. Empathetic listening is particularly important here.

A more probing approach from the start is likely if you have gone, or been referred to counselling because of debt and money problems. You may be asked to describe exactly what money means to you; why you seem to have such a need to overspend; why you can't live within your income. Then, together with the counsellor, you may be able to work out practical strategies to prevent huge debts piling up in future. This may mean looking closely at your budget to see which items might be excluded or cut down on. It may mean redoubling efforts to increase your income.

But before embarking on any specific strategies, you have to understand the deeper meaning of money – for you. For some people, it is simply a form of exchange. Most of us underestimate what we spend, because of fears surrounding finances. You may be asked to look at your fears over money, your supposed inability to manage it, and come to terms with why it causes so many problems in your life.

You may be working at a low-paid job because inwardly you don't feel you deserve better; you may be overspending because you feel cheated in some way; you may just not be earning enough to cover all your commitments. There may be many underlying reasons, a number of possible solutions; through counselling you should be able to arrive at one which works for you.

As you come to realize how thinking, feeling and behaving are intimately interconnected, the counsellor may help you in various ways to develop 'coping skills'. These 'skills' could involve learning deep breathing and specific relaxation exercises; doing role plays of a dreaded situation – perhaps going for a job interview, confronting your family, meeting your ex-lover; and practising positive thinking – telling yourself that you can cope, that this situation is not inherently frightening. For example, you may be so nervous of going to a social gathering that you either refuse the invitation, get sick on the day or spend the occasion in terror. Once you voice these fears, your counsellor may help you replace negative statements with positive ones, such as saying to yourself: Although I am anxious, I now have coping skills which I can use, and this is an opportunity for me to use them. Or you might say: I accept the anxiety and, using coping skills, I can feel the tension draining away.

Your counsellor may also remind you that every time you practise coping skills, just as every time you practise driving as a learner, fears diminish and confidence grows. An important aspect of counselling is encouraging you to face up to your fears, to do things although you may fear them (so long as the activity is not life-threatening or dangerous in itself). It is basically fear that brings most people to counselling -- and counselling works by helping clients to learn strategies for reducing whatever fears they may have.

At the end of the middle phase of counselling, whatever your problems are, you should have a clear idea of what they are, whether there is a recurring pattern, what childhood experiences have contributed to your present feelings and how your attitudes have affected your difficulties. You will not necessarily have resolved all, or any, of these problems but at least they will have been brought out into the open.

You may feel somewhat overwhelmed at the realization of what you imagined was a fairly straightforward temporary difficulty, such as being made redundant or being rejected for another partner, is actually part of an extremely complicated pattern of thought, attitude and behaviour on your part. You may appreciate that you sometimes sabotage your own efforts, that you have rationalized and denied, that you have made choices which, with hindsight, were not the best ones you might have made. You should have been able to see any recurring patterns in your life, if perhaps you seem to attract, say, weak and needy people to you, or appear to be 'accident-prone'. You should know if you carry a burden of rage against your parents, if you have difficulty in admitting feelings.

In other words, by the end of the middle phase of counselling, you should know yourself far better than you did before. Otherwise, you can be sure that your counselling has largely been a waste of time. The whole point of counselling is to get to know yourself and counsellors are trained (we hope!) precisely to facilitate this process of self-knowledge.

'Owning' What You Say

This is a very important aspect of counselling that is particularly associated with the middle phase. So what does it mean to 'own what you say'? At its simplest, to say 'I' instead of 'we', 'you' or 'one'.

An example of *not* fully owning what you say is the couple who talk of 'we' instead of 'I' when they are in fact referring to something individual. 'We enjoyed that film, didn't we, Cyril?' a wife may say. 'We believe all terrorists should be hanged,' a spouse may state in company. By using 'we' like this, the person can avoid standing alone in his or her opinions and feelings, can shift some of the personal responsibility for them.

Other people may disown the responsibility by depersonalizing everything and saying 'one' — 'One married, of course, thinking it was going to last for ever.' 'Of course, it's a great sadness when one's favourite dog dies.' Then there are people who say 'you', pushing the feelings away from themselves and onto the other person. 'Well, you would be angry, wouldn't you?' 'When you're made redundant, you feel as if the bottom has dropped out of your world.' 'When you try to pick up the pieces, you find it's more difficult than you ever imagined.'

Counsellors may well pick you up on your use of words such as 'we', 'one' or 'you' when you actually mean 'I'. It may come as a surprise to find how difficult the word 'I' can be to use, and to recognize the fears behind that. You may be encouraged to practise using it, boldly to say 'I' where you may have said we, or you, before. So instead of saying 'We enjoyed that film,' you will take responsibility for that statement and say: 'I enjoyed it.' If you have an opinion on capital punishment, you will say: 'I believe all terrorists should be hanged.' If you are upset at being made redundant, say: 'When I was made redundant, it was as if my world had fallen apart. I found it far more difficult to pick up the pieces than I had imagined.'

Next time you are watching television chat shows or interviews, notice how frequently − or infrequently − people are confident enough really to own what they say, fully to own their feelings. For example, Mrs Thatcher, commenting in a magazine interview about her reactions to being ousted from office, said 'you' all the time, not 'I'.

Using 'I', owning what you say, imparts a sense of responsibility and power. It means you are taking charge of your own life, risking the unknown with more confidence.

The End Phase

This is the phase when you and the counsellor are winding up your work together and it can sometimes be the most demanding of all. Depending on the agreed length of the counselling, the end stage may extend over differing periods, from one to many sessions. But you should always know in advance when the counselling is going to stop: any counsellor worthy of the name knows that endings, of whatever kind, are important and you need to have some time to adjust to them.

If the earlier sessions have worked, you will now feel you have got to know previously unfamiliar sides to yourself. You will have gained a new understanding and appreciation of the problem and have learned some strategies and skills to carry on. Many previous fears − fear of what other people might think, fear of rejection, fear of failure (or success), fear of looking silly or of being inadequate – should have been faced, brought out into the open and, if not entirely dissolved, at least much diminished.

Counsellor Jocelyn Chaplin, author of a number of books on counselling, says that people coming for counselling often experience a kind of symbolic death – the death of their old illusions. For many, the end phase of counselling is like scales falling from the eyes; suddenly, everything becomes clear. There may be a sense of wholeness, of having completed an exciting journey, rather like an exhilarating and slightly dangerous moutain climb.

But the loss of your old illusions will probably have brought pain and discomfort, and as counselling draws to an end you may have moments of doubt that you have reached your goal, that you have found more effective ways of dealing with difficult feelings. In the end phase of counselling, your counsellor will therefore aim to help you affirm and consolidate what you have achieved.

You will be encouraged to talk of changes in your feelings and behaviour, of how you now approach your relationships or work without feeling, for example, you must have approval and respect for everything you do, that you must complete every assignment perfectly; when you no longer fear being judged harshly and no longer judge others or have unrealistic expectations of them; when you no longer sabotage your own efforts and can treat yourself with self-respect.

At the end phase of counselling, your self-respect, self-esteem and self-confidence should have risen considerably. But don't expect to have complete self-confidence. You wouldn't be human if there were not still fears, still moments of doubt.

Where counselling has been over a long period, when a particularly close relationship may have developed between you and the counsellor, the end phase may concentrate on your feelings about the ending of this relationship, that out of the loss you can now grow, be independent. If you have gone to counselling because of a bereavement, the counsellor may well use the end phase to help you finally to let go of grief and move on alone with more confidence. But with all problems, loss of some kind is involved and the end phase is about you recognizing how you have gained and grown from it.

If the counselling has been effective, you – and no longer the counsellor – will at this stage be interpreting your own feelings and behaviour, using your newfound insights and putting them into practice in your personal and work relationships. Counsellors will be there in this end phase more to act as the final testing ground before you finally move off on your own. Their role is shortly to end and good counsellors will take satisfaction – one reason they're in the job – from you not needing counselling any more because, if it has worked, you are able to acknowledge your own true feelings, to understand why certain thoughts rise up in you from time to time, and to be positive and independent in your outlook.

At the end you should have reached your agreed goal – but this does not mean all your problems are solved. Even the most liberating counselling journey is no once and for all but a foundation for the remainder of life's journey. For many people, there may still be much sorting out to do. Where there has been a major trauma, such as child abuse, it may take years for the person to come to terms with it and all that counselling can hope to do in the short term is bring the problem out into the open. The person may then need help of a more specific kind, which the counsellor may suggest. In other cases, counselling may uncover such extensive problems that the client may want to move into more intensive therapy.

But counselling has worked for you if, after the agreed number of sessions, you have learned better and more positive ways of relating to people, you can accept and love yourself and others, and not seek to change other people. It has worked if you gain a renewed feeling of optimism and self-confidence, or when confidence and positivity have replaced a previous feeling of helplessness and despondency. It has worked if you no longer feel you are powerless, in the grip of forces you cannot control, if you no longer feel you are a victim of circumstances or that your life, for some indefinable reason, never seems to work out.

Life may not be all plain sailing after counselling – there will always be challenges, people may still not behave as you would like them to do, you may still be made redundant, your children may continue to disappoint you, relationships will not necessarily last or be endlessly fulfilling. But you will have greater personal means to deal with new problems as they arise or with old problems which may have bothered you for years. You will see not only yourself but everybody around you in a new light – colleagues at work, your friends, your parents, your children, your partner, your neighbours. It is as if before you saw through a glass darkly and now you are seeing things as they really are.

This does not mean that your actual circumstances will necessarily change dramatically; indeed, outwardly they may change very little or not at all. But you will be aware of having 'grown up', that you are now able to walk when you have only crawled before. You won't get so angry with yourself, you won't feel that you are less of a person because everything is not perfect all the time; you will have more courage to do what you really want to do, rather than being governed by other people's rules and scripts.

But it's not the counsellor's insights which have enabled these changes to take place – you have discovered them for yourself, and acted on them.

Effects on Others

Successful counselling doesn't just affect one person, it has ramifications for everybody around you. You may find that people encourage you in going to counselling; this may be especially true if your problem has been having very direct distressing effects on those close to you – as, for example, a husband and father with a heavy drinking problem who becomes aggressively drunk or a mother who is so severely depressed she can't face getting up. Alternatively, you may find your decision to go for counselling meets with hostility, or possibly indifference, from the beginning. But even when others see your counselling as something very positive, of benefit to them as well as you, they may well not be prepared for how the changes in you affect them.

Sometimes you will find that friends, family and work colleagues may resist the changes – they may say they preferred you as you were. Changing and growing is not always comfortable for others in your life – it may mean that they have to think about changing and growing, too. They may find it difficult to live with your new insights, your new serenity, your new propensity for owning what you say. Accordingly, they may denigrate counselling, out of their own fears.

You need to bear in mind that your counselling may be threatening to those close to you, who may have all sorts of fantasies of what goes on in this room from which they are excluded. A partner or parent, for example, may imagine you being encouraged to blame them, behind their backs, for your problem and the counsellor may seem to them a threatening figure siding with you against them. If you find yourself under fire in this way, you should be able to use your newfound abilities of not judging others, respecting their feelings, while holding to the benefits that you know you are finding for yourself in counselling. It is true that counselling will affect every single relationship you have – but the whole idea is to *improve* your relationships with others.

Your Relationship with the Counsellor

Much has been written about the relationship between the client/patient and the counsellor/therapist, from Freud onwards. And the debate continues. The theory of 'transference' – where patients attribute (or transfer) to the analyst their feelings stemming from past relationships – is central to the development of psychoanalysis and much modern therapy concerns the way transference (and counter-transference – the feelings aroused in the therapist by the patient) comes into the therapeutic relationship.

Counselling consciously avoids using theoretical labels but any good counsellor will be aware of the complex feelings that may be brought into the counselling room and affect the counsellor-client relationship. How much, if at all, your counsellor will make use of the transference theory varies according to the individuals and the type of counselling – counsellors working in the psychodynamic tradition (see next chapter) and over longer periods are going to be particularly aware of it. But in all counselling, the relationship between you and the counsellor is very important and it helps to know what feelings can be involved – and the professional boundaries which counsellors should not over-step.

Unlike in therapy or analysis, you are called the client and not the patient – a label deliberately avoided because of its implications of sickness to be treated by the expert, the doctor/therapist dispensing wisdom. The term client itself implies a greater equality and the counselling relationship is seen as one more of equals, with both of you embarking on a journey together. The counsellor does not know more about you than you know yourself – but she or he has learned certain skills to enable you to get to know yourself better.

The relationships should be empathic, friendly – but detached. Your counsellor is not a friend and won't – or certainly shouldn't – be revealing her or his personal circumstances, attitudes and opinions. Counsellors, in their training and their own therapy, are expected to reach an understanding of their own problems and feelings so that these do not get mixed up with those of the client and they are enabled to be empathic without getting identified with the client.

If you were to say: 'I had a terrible time being bullied at school', you will not want to know that the counsellor had a terrible time with the same problem, though you will of course want to know that the counsellor understands what you went through. You do not go to counselling to hear about the counsellor's experiences and if you feel that your counsellor is using you, as the client, for her or his own emotional purposes, wind up the sessions fast.

The special nature of the counselling relationship, at the same time both detached and intimate – this may well be the first time for many people that they have expressed such deep emotions to anyone – can lead to clients having strong feelings towards their counsellors, both positive and negative. There will almost certainly be ups and downs, times when you may feel irritated or angry with your counsellor, then maybe grateful and loving.

Good counsellors will accept such feelings and not be fazed by them. But counsellors are all human beings, with their own failings, difficulties and emotional problems. They are not automatons, their own feelings may well be deeply touched by what you tell them and it is unrealistic to expect them always to get it right or behave perfectly.

There are, however, certain boundaries which no counsellor should ever cross, of which the sexual boundary is the most obvious. This is not to say that sexual attraction should never come into the relationship – indeed it is not uncommon for clients to fall in love with their counsellors, nor for counsellors to be affected by sexual feelings for their clients, and this may sometimes be an important aspect of the relationship that needs to be worked through. But it does mean that sex with your counsellor can never, ever, constitute part of the therapeutic relationships, be part of healing, or justified in any circumstance.

The counsellor is in a position of trust as regards the client and should resist any implied or overt sexual behaviour. It is no defence that the client may have fallen in love, may have wanted a sexual relationship or may have enjoyed one if it happened. There is an old joke in counselling circles, where the client says: 'I find you really attractive. I'd like to go to bed with you.'

To this the counsellor replies: 'But we can't go to bed. I'm your counsellor.'

Client: 'You're fired as my counsellor. Let's go to bed.'

It is up to the counsellor to resist such a temptation. Like doctors, counsellors should be fully aware of the ethical implications of their position. The relationship is based on trust, and sexual intercourse or other overtly sexual behaviour is a betrayal of that trust – even if the client claims to see it differently. It not only cannot help the client towards independence, which is the ultimate goal of counselling, it does the opposite – by encouraging dependency, wrongly placed intimacy and a relationship that can never be healthy and equal.

The question of touch may, however, be different. Some modes of counselling encourage non-sexual touch, such as holding hands or even hugging. Generally, though, counsellors consciously do not use physical contact, believing that this can intrude on the relationship in a way that may curtail the client's freedom fully to express and 'own' their feelings.

The relationship should also not involve any socializing between counsellor and client. The counsellor is not a friend, not in the usual sense, and your relationship should be confined to the counselling room and end with the termination of counselling. If you happen to meet your counsellor between sessions, perhaps when out shopping or at a function, you may feel disconcerted, uncomfortable, even though you may also be pleased to see them. Counsellors will be aware that such 'outside' meetings can be difficult, if sometimes inevitable, and any counsellor who goes so far as to suggest, or agree to, social meetings is one to avoid. The relationship is then being put onto another footing and will no longer be of therapeutic value to you.

Knowing If It Has Worked

Professional counsellors Dave Mearns and Windy Dryden, authors of many handbooks on counselling methods, say that clients are often disappointed that everything is not wonderful after counselling, that there are still problems and difficulties, and still feelings of going three steps forward and two back. Counselling works by fits and starts – not by pulling you in a continuous upward direction. It can be hard work, both for you and the counsellor. You'll know you've been successfully counselled, though, if you now feel that you can cope better – whatever the circumstances – and that you have discovered personal strengths you didn't know you had.

If you feel exactly the same as you did before, if you feel that no light has been shed on your situation, if you feel there has been no clarity, then counselling has *not* worked for you. There may be several reasons for this.

It could be that you were not really ready to benefit from counselling, or that you were dragooned into going. Nowadays, employers sometimes send their staff for counselling when their work or behaviour with their colleagues seems to be unsatisfactory. Or your partner or doctor may have urged you to go for counselling and you have attended against your will. If you are not wholehearted about counselling, then it can never work – however expert, empathic or understanding the counsellor might be. If you are not interested in learning more about yourself, you will probably reject everything the counsellor says.

But lack of readiness or willingness to grow is not the only possible reason for failure. It may be that you and the counsellor simply do not hit it off. Counsellors obviously have individual personalities and there may be something just too incompatible for you to be able to work together. You may just not resonate.

Or it could be that the type of counselling you have chosen, or been sent to, simply does not suit you. There are now many different styles of counselling and counsellors work according to the one that they, personally, feel to be most effective. But this may not always be the most effective for you. In the next chapter we will look at the main styles of counselling, to help you decide which kind might be the one for you.

4

Different Styles of Counselling

As outlined in Chapter 1, present-day counselling grew out of a number of different schools of psychoanalysis and psychotherapy, and the counselling movement has developed to include a number of styles. Most counsellors adhere, at least to some extent, to one of these styles, which will affect the way they work, and it may help you to discover in advance which style your counsellor follows.

All counsellors, whatever their training and individual approach, aim to help you lead a more fulfilled life and are there to provide emotional support, clarification of difficult issues and a non-judgemental, accepting environment. But differences of counselling style may mean that one appeals to you more than another. It may be that one style feels more 'right' for you than another, even though you may not be able to put your finger on exactly why.

People tend to go to a particular counsellor because of a recommendation, perhaps by a doctor or friend, or after consulting agencies or source directories, when they will probably choose according to where they live (and what is available). But it is worth knowing that there are different counselling styles, each of which will have a bearing on how the counsellor approaches your particular problem. For example, a behaviourist-oriented counsellor may work from the viewpoint that at some stage in your life you have learned inappropriate forms of behaviour which need replacing with more effective behavioural patterns. The counsellor will therefore concentrate on your external behaviour rather than on possible unconscious motivations for it, as a counsellor working in the psychodynamic tradition probably would.

This chapter aims to give you a brief guide to the main styles of counselling in current use, with an indication of more 'fringe' styles you may come across, so that you can decide which might be for you. Broadly speaking, the counsellor training courses accredited by the British Association for Counselling take either a person-centred or a psychodynamic approach, but it is important to remember that there are no hard and fast divisions. Styles overlap and in practice, counsellors are likely to make use of theories and methods from a wide variety of sources.

Person-centred or Rogerian Counselling

Person- or client-centred counselling was developed by the American psychologist Carl Rogers and grew out of the humanistic approach of the 1950s, which basically sees humans as perfectible. It was also, to some extent, a rebellion against what was seen as the patriarchal, hierarchical, Central-European basis of traditional psychoanalysis. The aim was to remove the label of 'expert' from the therapist and put the client (never called a patient) firmly in charge; the relationship between the client and the counsellor should be equal and clients are considered to know as much as, if not more than, counsellors about their own problems. The humanistic approach is not so much concerned with pathological states such as neurosis and psychosis as the ordinary unhappiness and sense of alienation experienced at times by everybody.

Carl Rogers, who was originally a Christian evangelist training for the ministry, considered that traditional lengthy analysis was often not necessary to get to the heart of people's problems, and that verbal exchanges could work just as well, if not better. He believed that our basic human nature is positive, loving and peaceful but that early and later experiences may have clouded this. The client-centred approach, he believed, can help us to be aware of our true selves, when we will be able to move forward with confidence and love and a sense of connectedness with the world around us.

In order to facilitate the process of helping us to understand our true natures, the character of the counsellor is extremely important. It is not enough just to be accepting; the counsellor must also have empathy and what Rogers called 'unconditional positive regard' for the client, combined with 'congruence' or genuineness on the part of the counsellor.

It all sounds very nice, but Jeffrey Masson, a former Sanskrit scholar who later trained as a psychotherapist and still later, having researched the subject, decided that nobody outside oneself could genuinely be relied on to give useful help, wonders whether it is as altruistic and egalitarian as it is claimed. Masson, whose disillusion set in when he was allowed access to the Freud archives and decided that the father of psychoanalysis had hidden his findings on child abuse and led people to believe his patients were all fantasizing, gave up his analytical practice to become a writer and lecturer against therapy.

In his book *Against Therapy*, where he argues that all modern forms of therapy are flawed, he has this to say about Carl Rogers:

> It is unarguable that Rogers did away with some of the 'trappings' of the imbalance in the power relationship. He insisted on changing the designation 'patient' to 'client' which, being more mercenary, is closer to the truth. He called his method 'client-centred' (or person-centred), eschewing the labels of expert or specialist. He rejected the 'medical model of illness'. He was against all forms of manipulation of therapy.

His summing up of Rogers has a cynical tone and indeed Masson, who remains terminally angry about all therapists and therapies, wonders whether the 'unconditional positive regard' which Rogers says must be present in the good client-centred counsellor is actually possible. He feels that this kind of regard cannot be legislated or taught, any more than any other kind of love can, and that there is as much (or almost as much) scope for client abuse as with other types of therapy. Masson feels that empathy, on which Rogers places such emphasis, is singularly lacking in most kinds of therapy and that, at heart, therapists want to have power over their patients and bend them to their theories of human nature.

However, Masson reckons that the client-centred approach can do less harm than Freudian, Jungian or Kleinian approaches, all of which he believes have perpetrated more harm than good, because they put the therapist firmly in charge and encourage patients to believe that they are sick and need 'therapy', whereas it is more likely that society and current values are sick.

To further his case, Masson points out that until very recently those who complained of being abused as children were believed to be suffering from delusions and fantasy, rather than telling the truth. If psychiatry could get something as fundamental as this wrong for decades, Masson argues, what else might they be getting wrong? All therapies proceed on theories of human behaviour which may or may not be true. Indeed, whole edifices have been constructed on theories which, with hindsight, seem extremely questionable. Now that so much of traditional psychiatry has been discredited, how can we be sure that newer schools of thought, such as the human potential movement, of which client-centred counselling is a central part, are more accurate?

We can't – we can only believe that the proof of the pudding is in the eating. Rogers' view of humanity as essentially good, loving and peaceful accords directly with the teachings of all major religions and very many people who have come to client-based counselling have felt that it worked for them. This, objects Masson, may be quite meaningless, as all patients have a desire to believe that the medicine does them good, and the more painful, the better it must be doing them. Whatever the arguments, client-centred counselling is increasingly popular with people who are feeling unable to cope with everyday life and the challenges that ordinary events throw up.

In order to facilitate the client-centred approach, Rogers developed a technique known as 'mirroring' where the counsellor repeats back what the client has said. If, for example, the client says: 'So I went and thumped him one,' the counsellor may say: 'So you went and thumped him one.' The point of mirroring is to facilitate the clients' thought processes and make them aware of just what they have said. But clearly there is more to this kind of counselling than endless repetition by the counsellor.

The underlying idea is that, through the counsellor's acceptance, empathy, unconditional positive regard for the client, the client can gradually scour away at the layers of negativity which have been preventing them from being the kind of person they ought to be, which, according to Rogerian theory, is happy, successful, positive and at peace. The counsellor and the client both come to see how the client could be — and gradually, together, they work towards that goal. The emphasis will be on the present, the conscious thoughts of the client, rather than on unconscious processes or reconstructions of the past.

At the heart of the client-centred approach is the understanding that people act out of the way that they feel about themselves. People who are always having accidents, getting into work difficulties or failing in relationships would be seen as not valuing themselves very highly. Such people are basically co-dependent, which means they have an overwhelming desire for the love and regard of others, without ever knowing how to achieve this. They do not love themselves but want others to love them. There is progressive alienation from the true self, or the soul, and this can lead people to act in all kinds of self-destructive ways. They are the people who don't really know who they are. This does not mean that such people are necessarily shy or timid. They may be arrogant, bombastic, aggressive, outwardly self-assured.

The aim of the client-centred approach is to enable people to get back in touch with themselves again, to become 'fully functioning' and in touch with their own deepest feelings and responses. Rogerian counsellors believe that humans are basically unique, beautiful, positive, peaceful and that the counselling merely works to uncover this, to strip away the layers of doubt and denial. The main task of the counsellor is to create a climate of love and regard whereby people can start to flourish, possibly for the first time. The counsellor attempts to provide a different kind of soil than they have known before, whereby the plant can flourish instead of withering.

The main criticism of client-centred counselling is that it can be naive and optimistic, falsely idealistic and not making allowance for the negative side of human nature. Rogerian counsellors are said to see only the loving aspect of their clients, however the latter may seem to the outside world.

Psychodynamic Counselling

This form of counselling, which is the one taught by the British Westminister Pastoral Foundation, the biggest counselling and training service in the UK, grew mainly out of Freudian thought, although it has developed greatly from its early roots. Basically, psychodynamic counselling goes deeper than client-centred counselling and helps clients to understand unconscious motives for their actions and to bring these into conscious awareness.

Central to Freudian analysis is the idea that many of our conflicts and problems are a result of our unconscious motives and feelings, and that there is great resistance in bringing them to the surface. Psychodynamic counselling uses psychoanalytic techniques to enable clients to be aware of underlying motives and to bring repressed feelings and fears to the surface. Because it is related to psychoanalysis, some people may feel this type of counselling is more hierarchical than other kinds. Certainly, the counsellor here is seen as some kind of expert, although the old trappings of big important therapist and nervous little client have virtually disappeared from the psychodynamic approach.

The word 'psychodynamic' refers to the psyche – usually meaning the mind, emotions and spirit combined – which is seen as an active force, and not static. Activity, according to counsellors working in this way, can take place within the psyche, whether or not this bears any relation at all to what is going on in the outside world. The psyche seems to consist of a number of different selves, as in the saying: 'I'm not feeling myself today.' But, what is *myself*?

When people say they are not feeling 'themselves', this must mean that they believe there is another 'self' somewhere which is more true to how they really are.

The purpose of psychodynamic counselling is to help people uncover their true self – and be aware of the false ones. This means bringing unconscious material up to conscious levels and examining it closely. Counsellors will draw on analytical theories – for example, Freud's id, ego and superego, Jung's concepts of the anima, animus, shadow, Winnicott's true and false self – and will very much work on uncovering experiences and feelings in the past. Serious attention will also be paid to fantasies (or apparent fantasies), dreams and all the internal factors which contribute to dynamic forces or activities within the psyche.

The psychodynamically trained counsellor will be interested in understanding, or getting the client to understand, all the relationships involved in the psyche, and sorting them out. Because the unconscious is considered so important, counsellors who work in this way will be trying to understand how the unconscious motives of the client have affected their lives up to the present. Once unconscious motives can be brought out into the open, the idea is that clients will be able to act with more conscious control and awareness. The unconscious is unknowable, therefore it is likely to act in ways which are not helpful to us. The psyche is seen as a kind of prison which craves release and the object of psychodynamic counselling is to enable it to be released.

When counselling of this kind is successful, it helps the client to balance his or her own basic psychological needs, the demands of conscience, and the demands and external reality of particular situations. Repression leads to thoughts and feelings being denied and this means that life is not being lived fully in the present. Aspects of oneself are shut off, inaccessible to feeling and emotion because of what is going on in the unconscious. So the most important aspect of psychodynamic counselling is to help clients make sense of their current situations, to understand why they have got themselves in this particular state and to help them see that they can get themselves out of it.

Because psychodynamic counselling is complicated, and because it demands knowledge of Freudian, Jungian and other theories of the mind, such counsellors have to be very thoroughly trained. They also have to understand such concepts as transference, resistance and counter-transference, as all these are likely to crop up within the counselling relationship. If a client has a history of relating to important people in, say, submissive or aggressive ways, then this will be transferred to the counsellor -- and the counsellor has to be ready to deal with it. The counsellor can never make up to the client what he or she may have suffered in the past and there may be great disappointment when the client realizes that the counsellor cannot always provide the kind of guidance and advice that may be expected. Clients may feel rejected, especially if the counsellor has come to be seen as a kind of wise, ideal parent, and again counsellors have to be prepared for this and how to handle it.

Resistance is when the client resists attempts to bring repressed material to the surface, and counter-transference happens when the therapist unconsciously transfers her thoughts and feelings to the client. Clearly counsellors are working with deep emotional material here. Clients may express anger, rage, despair and depression during the sessions and counsellors have to know how to handle strong feelings, both their own and those of their clients.

The counsellor has to be able to listen carefully to what the client is saying and during the first session will make an assessment as to whether they can properly work together. A responsible counsellor will draw attention to the unpredictability of the outcome of counselling and will not make any false promises or give any expectation of a miraculous cure.

The counsellor needs to assess very carefully what counselling means to the client, why the client has come, what is hoped to be gained from the sessions. Because this approach may touch on fundamental disturbances in the psyche, particular attention will be paid to the client's past history, whether help has been sought elsewhere, whether the client is on any prescription or other drugs, ever been in hospital or treated by a psychiatrist, attempted suicide or other destructive behaviour.

During this and subsequent sessions, the client and counsellor will sit in chairs opposite each other. In this respect, psychodynamic counselling differs from traditional psychoanalysis, where the patient lies on a couch.

As with other types of counselling, the most important quality the counsellor brings to the sessions is listening ability. Clients are encouraged to talk about everything that is bothering them and the counsellor will usually remain relatively quiet. As with client-centred counselling, the client is considered to be in charge and the counsellor's aim is to provide clarification, to try to put into words what the client might be trying to express, but not to impose her or his own views or interpretations. Psychodynamic counsellors are, however, likely to take increasing account of how clients respond to the actual counselling relationship as the sessions continue, and look at the feelings aroused in the client by it.

According to Michael Jacobs, lecturer in Counselling Studies at the University of Leicester, and author of the book *Psychodynamic Counselling in Action*, this kind of counselling is not suitable for anybody who wants immediate answers or clarification. It tends to be long-term and can be particularly emotionally demanding of the client. As with other modern forms of counselling, the relationship has to be one of partnership, where the client collaborates in his own healing and growth. This can be a slow process, with many frustrations, where deep-seated problems are encountered.

Psychodynamic counsellors, unlike those working in the client-centred approach, believe that it is not enough just to provide a safe and loving environment, because it is considered that this will not necessarily help all the difficult negative feelings to come to the surface. Whereas the client-centred therapist puts the emphasis firmly on unconditional love and positive regard, the psychodynamic counsellor allows hate, anger and other negative feelings arising from loss and disappointment to come out, be expressed, acknowledged and validated. Through the counselling relationship, clients can relive and release their negative feelings and discover that they are allowed to have them.

According to Michael Jacobs, there is, however, unlikely to be a positive outcome to psychodynamic counselling unless clients have had at least one long, fulfilling and deep relationship in their lives. If there has been no such relationship, and there does not seem to be an ability to form one, then the client may well not be able to respond to the counsellor-client relationship, which is essentially an intimate association, with all the elements of transference, love, projection, denial, resistance, associated with a close relationship.

All counsellors need to know how to deal with difficult situations as they crop up, to be aware of the need for detachment while still staying close to client's emotions. But psychodynamic counsellors perhaps in particular must have had rigorous training to avoid the risk of both client and counsellor floundering helplessly in the mire of hidden thoughts and motives being brought to the surface.

Most modern training courses for counsellors rely on either client-centred or psychodynamic counselling, or a mixture of both. Many of the styles described below have derived input from these two approaches, just as the latter may adopt some aspects of other styles. Modern counselling is often eclectic in approach. The behaviourist style, however, stands more on its own.

Behaviourist Counselling

The behaviourist method grew out of dissatisfaction with standard psychotherapy and has been developed mainly by Hans Eysenck, for many years Professor of Psychology at the Institute of Psychiatry, and his fellow workers. Eysenck questioned whether psychoanalysis could ever, or had ever, done any good. Even Freud, said Eysenck, admitted that analysis merely turned neurotic people into mildly unhappy people.

The behaviourist approach concentrates soley on symptoms, on what can actually be seen, rather than considering underlying causes which, it stresses, can only be guesswork – and we might have got it completely wrong. What we can know, however, is that, for whatever reason, people are afraid of flying, nervous of going out of the house, have a compulsion to collect and tidy things, or are terrified of spiders.

As, according to behavioural theory, we can only guess at how these problems arose in the first place, then working on the unconscious or childhood traumas may or may not hold the key to the solution. And certainly, any therapist or counsellor who has worked with serious phobias will know that, mostly, the reasons for the great fear are not uncovered during therapy sessions – they remain mysterious.

The behavioural approach, therefore, works only in the present and concentrates on helping clients to overcome and modify unhelpful behaviour by replacing it with more functional and less fearful ways of coping. The particular ritual or phobia will first be closely studied by the counsellor, then together, counsellor and client will try to work out ways of overcoming that behaviour. Behavioural counselling is very much goal-orientated, in that it will work solely towards the client being able to face that threatening situation and cope with it.

There are two specific strategies commonly used. One is 'laddering', where the client is taken step by step through the fearful situation. With a fear of flying, this may involve going to the airport, watching planes take off and land, stepping onto the runway, stepping on to a plane and, eventually, going on an actual flight. The other method often used is 'flooding', where the client is put in the frightening situation at once, thrown in at the deep end, and is surprised to survive it without mishap. Of course, behavioural counsellors should never put clients in any genuinely dangerous situations, such as literally throwing them in at the deep end, if they have a fear of water, when they can't swim.

Although behavioural counselling does not look at root causes of dysfunctional behaviour, it can be extremely useful when the phobia or ritualistic behaviour, such as compulsive handwashing or checking, is preventing people from living a full and active life. Since its introduction during the 1950s as part of the treatment given to patients in psychiatric hospitals, it has been very influential in the counselling movement and elsewhere. It is now used, for example, on Outward Bound courses, where adults are made to do what they fear – in order to overcome not only that particular fear but fears in everyday life as well. The idea is that by overcoming the phobias that are restricting life, fears can vanish and be seen for what they are – paper tigers.

Behavioural-type counselling can be considered by people who suffer from panic attacks, fear of public speaking, fear of making fools of themselves in public, paralysing shyness, persistent lateness, fear of flying, nervousness about getting on a bus or going to a party, fears about the outside world being contaminated or unhygienic – and who wish to overcome these problems. It has also had success with people wanting to give up smoking.

If not treated, phobias tend to get worse as the years go by, until people may be so completely hemmed in by their fears they can no longer do anything at all. Behavioural counselling works on the understanding that people get rewards of some kind for their behaviour. For instance, those who daren't go out of the house never have to take responsibility for their lives; those who have to enact complicated rituals and checking routines do this to make them feel safer and more secure.

The eventual aim of behavioural counselling is to enable people to become aware that there can be greater rewards for letting go of the phobic behaviour. Their behaviour will be modified in the right direction, according to the theory, when the rewards for functional behaviour are seen to be greater than those for the phobic attitudes.

Co-Counselling

Co-counselling, also known as Re-evaluation Counselling, was developed by American therapist John Heron as the ultimate in non-authoritarian counselling. The idea is that client and counsellor interchange roles and spend an equal amount of time counselling and being counselled.

Before becoming a co-counsellor, people attend a course, run by a group leader, where the basic premises of co-counselling are explained.

Co-counselling partners are not always the same: most people in co-counselling find that they can work with a number of different partners. The relationship is supposed to be that of equals, loving but detached partners. This means that intimate liaisons are not encouraged through the co-counselling network. There is touch, and hugging – seen as a very important aspect of the therapeutic process – but this must remain non-sexual.

Co-counselling is intended for those who wish to be more effective in their lives, rather than people who have deep-seated problems which they cannot seem to address or solve. It is a way of relating better to other people, and also to oneself. The fundamental premise behind it is that we are all basically good, loving intelligent people and that if we cannot respond to others, if we are negative, if we have low self-esteem, this is because of some hurt we suffered in early life, which has clouded our vision and our judgement.

The idea is that, through co-counselling, we will be able gradually to strip off the layers of negativity and reveal the intelligent, loving, positive person beneath. If there is incompatibility with other people, according to the co-counselling philosophy, this is most probably because of early distress. Through pairing off, we can learn to lose our fear of others and also our inhibitions. We can learn to trust other people more and also gain the confidence to face up to the source of our early distress.

Peter Clark, a psychotherapist and former university professor, teaches Fundamentals of Co-Counselling at London University. He says: 'Basically, co-counselling is a method of self-development which can help people improve their relationships with others.

'For most of us, the greatest problems in life spring from our interpersonal relationships. Co-counselling can show people how to be assertive rather than aggressive; it can teach people both how to listen and be listened to, and it can allow a situation where you can trust others not to betray or hurt or insult you.

'Many of us have established patterns in our lives where we are always putting either ourselves or other people down, and we have also established habits which are self-sabotaging rather than helpful.

'Co-counselling can work to change these negative patterns, and substitute them with more positive ones.'

The Fundamentals course lasts for a total of fifty hours and does not train people to be professional counsellors. Instead, it gives a chance for everybody to counsel and be counselled by a number of different people, so that they can see what it feels like to be on each side. Students on the Fundamentals courses may also find that they click with some people better than others – part of the value of co-counselling is trying to discover why. Very often, if we take an instant dislike to somebody or find a habit or particular trait in them annoying, it is because we have the same habit or trait ourselves, without realizing it. And when people make us angry, this is usually because they have touched some deep-seated but often unacknowledged emotion in us, an emotion we have perhaps buried. The person who makes us angry often holds up a mirror to our own true selves – and through co-counselling we can come to realize this.

There are three basic areas addressed in co-counselling: relationships, work and lifestyle. Most people cannot work their problems out on their own and they need some kind of help. But they may not need the sort of help that a professionally trained counsellor can give. This form of counselling is not considered suitable for people who are trying to cope with so much distress of their own that they are actually unable to listen to other people, nor is it for those who need actual psychiatric care.

It is for 'ordinary' people who wish to become more effective in their relationships with others, and also get to know themselves a bit better. As with other forms of counselling, though, painful, long-buried issues may come up which cause distress and which are difficult to discharge.

Co-counselling proceeds on the Rogerian basis that everybody, without exception, is loving, co-operative, zestful and intelligent. Through talking to a 'friend' it becomes possible to discharge early hurts and learned negative habits, to reveal the wonderful person beneath, the person who has been trapped for years in a destructive cycle of behaviour. Co-counselling provides a way of doing this without the expense and length of time that other forms of counselling may involve.

During co-counselling, emotional discharge, such as crying, trembling, raging, is encouraged on the grounds that such discharge aids healing. When adequate emotional discharge can take place, according to John Heron, the person is 'freed from the rigid behaviour and feeling left by the hurt. The basic loving, co-operative, intelligent and zestful nature is then free to operate.

'Such a person will tend to be more effective in looking out for his or her own interests and the interests of others, and will be more capable of acting successfully against injustice.'

It is understood that it can be dangerous for this emotional discharge to take place without counsellors knowing what they are handling, which is why a proper course is considered vital. As counselling partners get to know each other, the process begins to work better and better – and true re-evaluation can take place. All emotions must be discharged in a safe environment, which is why co-counselling is quite different from merely talking to a friend, who may collude with and encourage the negativity.

Often, those who have been in a co-counselling network come to find that they hit very deep or painful issues which cannot seem to be sorted out by the co-counselling methods. Therefore, this kind of counselling can lead on to more formal types of counselling or psychotherapy.

Gestalt Counselling

Gestalt (the word is German for 'form') was, like so many offshoots of psychoanalysis, developed in America in the 1960s. It was introduced at Esalen, the famous community founded in 1962 at Big Sur, California, and is still going strong.

Gestalt's originator was Berlin-born Fritz Perls, who was trained as a Freudian psychoanalyst and became Psychologist-in-Residence at Esalen. Many of the terms we are now familiar with, such as 'here and now', 'awareness' and 'the wisdom of the body' come from the gestalt concept, which basically holds that we should concentrate on what is happening now rather than trying to rake up the past, in order to find out who we really are and to take charge of our thoughts and actions.

The idea is that becoming more 'aware' can in itself facilitate important change and growth. In order to access this awareness, the concept of the 'hot seat' was developed, whereby one person sits in a chair and responds in various ways to other members of the group. Gestalt sessions can also be held on a one-to-one basis, where the client may be talking to an empty chair, saying what he or she would like to say to somebody, and then playing the part of the person responding.

The basic tenets of gestalt can be summed up as concern

with the present rather than the past; dealing with the present rather than the past; and accepting no 'should' or 'ought', other than your own. In other words, you take full responsibility for your actions, feelings and thoughts, and never blame anybody else for what has happened to you. In gestalt counselling the primacy of feelings is acknowledged and there is no idea of reliving or replaying old traumas and wounds in order to release them.

Although gestalt has many critics and, according to Jeffrey Masson, has to rely on a guru-type figure to lead the group or individual sessions, its philosophy has passed into the language and has become one of the cornerstones of the modern American growth movement. The famous gestalt 'prayer' goes:

> I do my thing and you do your thing.
> I am not in this world to live up to your expectations.
> And you are not in this world to live up to mine.
> You are you and I am I.
> And if by chance we find each other, it's beautiful.
> If not, it can't be helped.

Although there may be few hardline gestalt therapists working as counsellors, or using the specific techniques developed by Fritz Perls to heighten awareness, many counsellors will use at least some of the ideas in their approach. The gestalt prayer, although it now sounds rather Sixties, has helped to bring about a change in attitude towards relationships which is only now seeping into counselling work with alcoholics, drug addicts, people with eating disorders and so on.

The idea of the 'enmeshed' family, where members have no real sense of their own identity and have no clear concept of where they end and somebody else begins, is now seen as highly dysfunctional. It has been shown that people who identify too closely with others have little sense of their own separate reality – and gestalt ideas have helped people to try and stand alone, to take full responsibility for their actions and to see that each one of us is unique, separate and individual.

Gestalt therapists often work with groups, rather than on an individual basis, and many modern workshops and group therapy sessions have been influenced by the movement. It has been condemned in some circles as trying to lead to 'instant enlightenment' and 'instant awareness' but certainly the Esalen Centre is still flourishing in California and the gestalt approach continues to have an influence on counselling methods.

Transactional Analysis (TA)

This is another of the famous American 'growth' movements and its philosophy is embedded in the best-selling book by Eric Berne, *Games People Play*. The 'games' are the comfortable, unthinking roles people adopt in relation to certain circumstances or events. Each of us, according to the theory, contains within us the 'child', 'parent' and 'adult', and these states are constantly warring. For example, when we behave as the demanding 'child', this may not evoke the wanted 'parent' response in the other person. The 'child' in us wants immediate gratification and sulks if this is not available; the 'parent' in us is stern and adheres to the belief system instilled in us by actual parents, teachers and other authority figures, whereas the 'adult' aspect is analytical and self-aware.

The TA words, child, parent, adult, correspond closely to Freud's id, ego and superego, and can almost be seen as another means of saying the same thing. The purpose of TA is to try to access the real personality behind the apparent roles and in this way the movement has much in common with gestalt. American psychiatrist Eric Berne, founder of TA, believed that we all use various roles to try to avoid facing up to the real 'us'. We may hide behind real or assumed roles and come to believe these are actually 'us' when they are not. For instance, a woman may see herself as a 'wife and mother', identifying so closely with these roles she confuses them with herself. A man may see himself as a 'doctor' or 'politician', not realizing that these are merely roles which can at any time be taken away.

As TA concentrates mainly on helping people to improve their relationships with other people, the counsellor's attention will be focussed on interactions with close family members, colleagues or partners. Counsellors who use TA techniques will try to get the client to understand the various ego states within the personality and how these interact with each other, for good or ill. With understanding, comes awareness of how the various roles and games people assume and play are used to gain attention in various ways. Attention-gaining behaviour is known in TA parlance as 'strokes'.

The basic aim is to release the 'adult' within and separate it from the 'child' and the 'parent', so that we can bring our actions, thoughts and feelings into conscious awareness. TA work often takes place in groups, when people may be asked to set goals for changing their behaviour. But the concept may be used by counsellors working in more traditional styles, whose clients can be helped to realize when their 'child' comes out, when the 'parent' is in control and when the 'adult' is taking over instead.

Reichian Therapy and Bioenergetics

Reichian followers concentrate on the body rather than the mind, on the assumption that many old traumas and difficulties are held in the body, possibly for very many years. The longer they have been held in the body, the less likelihood there is that they will disappear of their own accord, as they have become 'fused' with us and seem to be part of us. Also called bioenergetics, Reichian therapy focuses particularly on bodily movements, breathing and body processes.

It is an offshoot of Freudian psychoanalysis developed in Vienna by Wilhelm Reich, who took Freud's idea that sexuality was at the root of many human problems even further and postulated that the cause of many difficulties and diseases, both mental and physical, was inability to achieve proper orgasm. He believed that regular orgasm helped the person to release problems by going temporarily out of control.

Like many pioneers, Reich himself had a thorny path through life. His mother committed suicide when he was fourteen after her teenage son informed his father that she was having an affair. He joined the Communist party after emerging from a Swiss sanatorium following a breakdown but was expelled in 1933 for his extreme ideas. He spoke out against current laws concerning homosexuality, birth control and abortions and was thought to be dangerous and subversive.

A former disciple of Freud, Reich moved to America, where he founded the Orgone Institute, and claimed to have invented an 'energy accumulator' which could cure cancer. He was sent to prison for refusing to dismantle these accumulators, as the US Food and Drug Administration demanded, and died in prison in 1957.

The idea behind the kind of therapy he developed was to dissolve the body 'armour' – the defences we have put up – in order to release repressed emotions and desires. New energies would become available when we no longer needed this armour and our lives could proceed more healthily than before and achieve their full potential. We would also be releasing long-held fears through this form of therapy, Reich believed, and activate 'orgone energy'.

In order to release the body 'armour', such techniques as breathing exercises and massage are used. During therapy, clients may kick, scream or otherwise become deeply emotionally affected by what is going on. Reichian bodywork was extremely popular in the 1960s and 1970s, and was used as a basis for the kind of mass sexual intercourse that took place at the late Bhagwan Shree Rajneesh's ashram in Poona. Later, in the age of AIDS, Rajneesh repudiated this form of therapy but it has entered into the consciousness of our age, so that many people still believe that sexual activity can release long-held emotions, repressions and fears, and that frequent orgasms can keep us healthy. Indeed, 'becoming orgasmic' is now seen as an extremely healthy sign and many books based on Reichian ideas (for example *The New Joy of Sex*) have been written to try to help us do just that.

Few modern Reichian therapists would go as far as the excesses of the 1960s and 1970s but the idea that the body can hold anger, fear and other emotions for many years and lead to illnesses and disorders has become accepted by many alternative and complementary practitioners. 'Bodywork' is now seen to be valuable in helping people to relax and release stress, so this form of therapy may suit people who feel they would prefer to work with the body, rather than simply trying to explore the mind and emotions through talking.

Psychosynthesis

Psychosynthesis aims to bring together all aspects of an individual's personality and help people towards a healthy, harmonious whole, rather than having warring parts which mean that full potential and inner peace can never be reached. It draws on the main tenets of Western psychology, together with some ancient Eastern ideals, such as the search for one's higher self, or higher consciousness.

The movement was founded by Roberto Assagioli, an Italian psychiatrist, who felt it was healthier to concentrate on establishing harmony in the personality, rather than delving into the hidden reasons for disorder and dysfunction. His view was that nature is always tending towards harmony and that therapy should help people to integrate aspects of themselves to discover the harmonious whole.

The British Psychosynthesis and Education Trust defines its aims thus:

> Psychosynthesis aims to build a personality which is free from emotional blocks, has command over all its functions and a clear awareness of its own centre. On the transpersonal level, it enables the individual to explore those regions full of mystery and wonder, beyond our ordinary awareness, which we call the superconscious, the wellspring of higher intuitions, inspirations, ethical imperatives and states of illumination.

Assagioli believed that it was impossible to control certain thought or behaviour patterns by an act of will. It was the imagination which was required to set new thought patterns in progress and in order to further the integration of all aspects of the personality, therapists and counsellors may make use of painting, diary writing and body movement.

The idea is that you will be guided through four distinct phases, which cover: a thorough knowledge of your own personality (many people *think* they know what they are like, but may be surprised to discover the 'real' person lurking beneath the layers); control and understanding of the various elements and layers; realizing your true self; and the actual 'psychosynthesis' – constructing the new, and more viable, personality now that you have found your true self.

Psychosynthesis can be particularly helpful in treating phobias, those irrational fears which are quite unrelated to an actual event. For instance, most people who are nervous of flying have never been involved in an aircrash, those who are frightened of spiders have never been harmed by them and individuals who hate sharp knives have never been stabbed or cut by one.

Modern counselling courses often include a course in psychosynthesis, and counsellors working in more mainstream styles may well make use of some of the techniques.

Psychodrama

This is a flourishing form of therapy, often part of residential counselling programmes, and can be a powerful way of releasing deep-seated problems and difficulties. The idea is that, with a skilled leader, we can 'act out' these problems because they have meant we are playing a part and not being true to ourselves. Through the 'acting', we can come to see what is really us and what are the superimposed roles we have been assuming – and the differences between them.

Psychodrama was founded by Jacob Moreno, who became a psychiatrist in Vienna. He became interested in what happened to actors and actresses in their private lives when they were playing certain parts on stage; he discovered, for example, that one actress became bitchy and difficult in real life when playing sweet, nice roles and the opposite when she was given bitchy parts to play.

He believed that psychodrama could become an important aspect of psychotherapy and he developed a number of techniques, all connected with the stage. There is 'soliloquy', where people describe their feelings in connection with a disturbing event such as the death of a close relative; 'mirroring', where somebody else tries to express the emotions another performer cannot release or express; and 'role reversal', where one person actually tries to become another.

The idea is that the spontaneity and creativity remove inhibitions, and empathy with others is developed. People are brought back in touch with their feelings, so that they find it easier to relate to other people.

Hypnotherapy

This is a method of counselling and therapy whereby people are encouraged under hypnosis to remember early experiences, so that these can be assimilated into the present, then discharged and released so that they can no longer exert a harmful influence. It is known that people tend to block out painful memories, which may become so deeply buried that they will not come out through ordinary talking. It is also known that no memory, however early, is ever really forgotten. Somewhere, it remains and will continue to exert a strong effect on subsequent behaviour and attitudes.

Many people fear they will be 'taken over' in hypnosis, that they may not be able to come out of the trance or that the hypnotist is an evil Rasputin who just wants to have his wicked way. In fact, although hypnosis is open to abuse, it is a time-honoured way of enabling people to bring deeply buried memories and traumas to the surface. Freud originally used hypnosis, after he came to understand that most problems would not go away until their root cause had been discovered and brought to conscious awareness.

Freud's later disillusionment with hypnosis as a tool was a major reason to its falling into disrepute early this century. But now it is coming back as its usefulness in treating various problems is increasingly recognized. Doctors and dentists have found it useful for patients whose dread of treatment is so great that, if they ever reach the surgery, they may run out screaming before any treatment has started. Medical and dental hypnosis is not of course strictly relevant to counselling but is part of the wider application of hypnotic techniques which may occasionally be used by therapists and counsellors. Hypnotherapy is commonly used, for instance, to help people give up smoking, lose weight or cope with public speaking. It has also been successfully used with childbirth and with some stress-related diseases, such as irritable bowel syndrome.

Hypnotic regression may be particularly helpful in unblocking memories of early traumas, such as child abuse, and with phobias of all kinds. Phobias are notoriously difficult to treat but through hypnosis it can come out that a phobia originated in some traumatic early experience.

Sometimes it may seem that this dates back to birth, or, according to some practitioners, it may have started earlier, in a previous incarnation.

Practising hypnotherapist Ursula Markham, author of many books on the subject, maintains that hypnosis is a skill which can be learned, rather than a gift which very few people possess. It is now possible to learn hypnosis on specialist courses and one indication of how seriously it is being taken is that at least one university, Sheffield, now has a recognized hypnosis course for doctors and dentists.

So what happens during hypnotic regression? You need not fear that you will be put into a trance – it is accepted that nobody can be hypnotized against their will and most hypnotists nowadays use only a very light form of trance, where you will remember everything that is being said, both during and after the session.

The most important aspect of successful hypnosis is the ability to relax. Unlike other forms of modern counselling, you may well be lying down on a couch or bed, covered with a blanket. Some hypnotists work with clients in chairs but relaxation is usually easier when lying down. It is the hypnotist's job to relax you, although you as the subject must be prepared to co-operate. If you are resisting the hypnotist, you will get nowhere. Different hypnotists have their own methods of relaxation but usually they will proceed by suggesting to you that gradually you are becoming more relaxed. The more esoteric hypnotists may also use crystals.

The preliminary consultation will have given the therapist some idea of why you have come – perhaps a phobia, such as fear of flying, or an awareness that you suffered from abuse as a child and want to get to the bottom of it or a problem with stammering, lack of confidence, or amnesia about certain times in your life.

The therapist will gently try to take you back to the time when the problems appeared to start by asking lots of questions, but she or he should never make suggestions to you. Everything must come from you, as the client. Part of the regression will mean reliving the experience which appears to have caused the present problems. Sometimes, one or two sessions will be enough to bring the experience out into the open, into conscious awareness and enable an adult perspective to be put on the situation. But where problems are very deep-seated, such as abuse which went on for years, it may take many more sessions.

So how can you know whether you are telling the truth, using your imagination, or maybe remembering a story you heard when young? How can you tell you are not simply wishing to impress the hypnotist or are not making up terrible events just to give yourself some sense of importance?

The answer is that you can never be really sure. But experienced hypnotists say that when genuine events are being recalled, there is always strong emotion present; if events being described were simply fantasies, simply products of the imagination, there would not be the accompanying emotion. As with any other form of counselling, the proof of the pudding is in the eating. If the phobias and blocks have cleared, then the therapy has been successful.

Hypnotherapy certainly does not work for everybody – and as with other forms of counselling, you have to feel ready to deal with whatever might come up as you may have no idea in advance.

A Case History

Stephanie kept thinking about her childhood and her bad relationships with her parents. For several years she had never even spoken to her mother. Also, she was bothered because she couldn't seem to pass her driving test, in spite of many lessons and numerous attempts. She decided to try to sort it all out and went to see a hypnotherapist who had been recommended to her as an expert in enabling people to relive and release very bad experiences from their past.

Through hypnosis, Stephanie gradually remembered a traumatic event which had happened to her at the age of six. When she was supposed to be looking after her younger sister, aged four, she had let her run out into the street, where she was knocked down by a car. Although badly injured, her sister survived. Stephanie had had no conscious memory of this event, which she had completely blocked out. She came to realize, through the hypnotherapy, that her inability to learn to drive or pass her test – which was seriously hampering her career as a music teacher – was connected with this childhood event. All her life, she had blamed herself for this incident – never mind that a child of six was not old enough to take responsibility for a younger sister – and the guilt feelings had meant that she had unconsciously continually sabotaged herself.

Stephanie said after her hypnotherapy: 'I was absolutely amazed that there was a reason why I could not seem to learn to drive, something just about everybody else I know can do without any problems. I had always had an ambivalent attitude towards my younger sister – perhaps I subconsciously wanted to kill her through jealousy and felt ashamed of this.

'It was all revelation to me but as it was all coming out, I definitely felt that it hit the spot. For the first time, genuine reasons for my attitudes and behaviour in adult life were coming out.

'I may be wrong, but I don't think that all this could have been accessed through other forms of counselling. It had been too deeply suppressed for that. Until the memory was reactivated through hypnosis, I had no recollection whatsoever of this accident.'

'Past Life' Therapy

Hypnotic regression which includes regression to possible past lives is also becoming popular, although most counsellors would certainly dismiss it as something definitely beyond the bounds of genuine treatment. Many hypnotists, however, have discovered the existence of past lives through accident, when, under hypnosis, their clients have spontaneously described lives which have no reality in the present.

There is considerable scepticism as to whether past lives recalled by hypnosis can be genuine. Detractors maintain that either the hypnotist is putting ideas into the person's mind or the client's imagination is working overtime. Dr Roger Woolger, a Jungian analyst who now specializes in past-life therapy, says that one way he can often tell whether clients' past lives are genuine or made up is that the genuine ones are usually so boring! Other hypnotherapists using past-life therapy say the same – the exciting, adventurous lives are very much in the minority. Also, as with recalling past events in the present, strong emotions are evoked by the memories, which would probably not be there if the subject was simply remembering a historical film or book.

But whether or not past lives are 'real' or 'fake', hypnotherapists are finding that this approach can help with deep-seated problems when all other approaches have left the problem untouched. The client is left with the feeling that his life now makes more sense. If you are interested in this type of therapy, it is essential to go to somebody you feel you can trust, because neither you nor the hypnotist will know in advance exactly what will come up.

Psychic Counselling

Psychic counsellors are supposed to be able to 'intuit' what a person's problem is and also to see a pattern which may have eluded the client. Some of them, but by no means all, also practise as mediums – people who purport to be able to contact the dead. Being a psychic means in fact nothing more than having very strong empathy with other people, the ability to tune into their wavelength without difficulty.

With psychic counselling, the long rigmarole of the beginning, middle and end of counselling, the problems of transference, counter-transference and resistance, are not encountered. The psychic possesses the (apparent) ability to enter into your mind and speak it for you. The work does not all have to come from you.

Most people who go to psychic counsellors have suffered bereavement or terrible loss with which they cannot come to terms. Previous unbelievers will often go to see whether they can be helped to get in touch with the dead person, to hear whether there are any last messages that will give them hope and make them feel better. There is often a pathetic hope that the dead person may not really be dead – and any apparent communication will be taken as a sign that the psychic has a genuine ability to contact dead people.

Partly because of the extreme vulnerability of most of the people it attracts, psychic counselling is viewed with serious doubts. The British Association for Counselling does not have any accredited psychic counsellors, nor does it ever recommend this type of counselling.

Psychic counselling, however, could be said to be the most ancient form of counselling in existence and for thousands of years before Freud, Jung, Rogers or any other modern analysts or therapists existed, people would seek help from those considered to have psychic powers. Help from psychic sources fell into disrepute in the Western world as Christianity gained a foothold and was virtually wiped out with the coming of the scientific age. However, paradoxically, science came to the aid of psychic matters in 1882, with the formation of the Society for Psychical Research, founded by a group of Cambridge scientists to conduct scientific, rational investigations into supposed psychic matters.

The researches of the SPR have shown beyond all possible doubt that some information may be relayed to us without the mediation of the five senses; in other words, the 'sixth sense' is a real phenomenon. Countless mediums and psychics have been investigated over the years by the SPR and although many have been exposed, some have appeared to have powers which defy any rational explanation.

Over recent years, there have been many investigations of mediums; can they really contact the dead, are they making it up, or what? Investigations carried out in‸ɔ the work of the late Doris Stokes, for instance, found that much of her supposed paranormal insight was information that she could have deduced by ordinary means.

But although we can't know whether supposed mediums are in contact with dead spirits, or whether there are such things as dead spirits, the fact is that bereaved people can be enormously comforted by such help.

The danger is that people tend to be extremely gullible when faced with a severe difficulty in their lives and tend to clutch at straws. They are open to exploitation, emotionally and financially. Sooner or later the loss has to be faced; it can't be magicked away. Unlike other types of counsellor, psychics may tell you what you are thinking; they may suggest things, put ideas into your head and outline possible strategies for the future. Fraudulent, or at best irresponsible, psychic counsellors may tell all their clients they are going to be rich and famous, meet a wonderful man or woman, and have a happy life thereafter. Others may predict trouble for the future. *Avoid all such people*. Nobody, whether purporting to be psychic or not, should ever attempt to foretell your future.

Good psychic counsellors, however, are aware that the best they can do is to help you put things into perspective, give you some indication as to why your life has become so difficult and suggest ways that things might be improved in future. As with other counsellors, they will encourage you to take responsibility for your own life, to substitute positive for negative ways of thinking, to achieve greater harmony with the universe, with your fellows, with your work and with your money.

Although most people visit psychics and mediums after suffering a bereavement, this is not the only type of loss or difficulty for which psychic counsellors offer help. For instance, parents who have a handicapped child may feel intense guilt, that they have done something to bring an infliction on them. Most psychic counsellors believe in the law of karma, the universal law of cause and effect, which says that every action must inevitably have a consequence. A child will have been born handicapped because of past karma, according to the psychic interpretation, and nothing anybody could have done would have made any difference.

For experiences which seem to have no rhyme or reason at all, it can be enormously comforting to see a psychic counsellor. But they don't know all the answers, any more than any other type of counsellor, and of course, the whole area of psychic matters is difficult to assess objectively.

Feminist Counselling

This approach to counselling has not grown out of any particular school, so much as the consciousness-raising feminist groups and feminist scholarship of the past decades. At its heart is the view that the hierarchical, patriarchal structures which govern our present Western society make it difficult for women to grow and flourish of their own accord. It is therefore intended especially to help women, who may often have doubts about going to coun-selling or therapy because they fear meeting hierarchical and patriarchal attitudes – after all, most schools of therapy have been developed by men or from male theories about the world.

The term 'feminist' is not an exact one – any more than are the other terms used in the counselling context – but can be taken to mean that the woman's view of things should be given serious consideration. In the context of feminist counselling, this means to be co-operative rather than competitive, to be supportive and sisterly rather than running each other down, to come together rather than be isolated, to harmonize with nature rather than working against it, to have a high regard for oneself, to be able to look after oneself, one's body and also the environment, to work for equality of relationships, and the ending of oppression for all, whether because of gender, race or ability levels. Feminist counselling tries to show that the emotions and the spirit are at least as important as what goes on inside the head, the rational and logical, analytical aspect of humans.

The main aim, as with any other kind of counselling, is to enable clients to develop self-confidence and to empower them to make proper choices and take responsibility for their lives. There will be non-judgemental acceptance of the client's attitudes, even where these are at variance with feminist theory. For example, a woman coming to feminist counselling may believe that a woman's place is in the home, being subservient to a husband. Although the feminist counsellor will not personally agree with this, she must accept the client's reality at the same time as trying to help the client uncover the reasons for her present unhappiness.

The counsellor should not have expectations, or give specific advice. The idea, says feminist counsellor Jocelyn Chaplin, is that the counsellor does not mind what the client does – the client's behaviour does not reflect back on the therapist. She does not, or should not have, a vested interest in the client's achievements. Feminist counselling thus does not depart from the client-centred approach described above in any radical way. Both indeed grew out of the humanistic movements of the 1950s and 1960s.

Most feminist counsellors will have undergone a standard period of counselling training and the feminist aspect will be an 'add-on'. Depending on the training of the counsellor, there may be work with dreams, with early childhood experiences, with attitudes, as well as presenting problems such as whether to leave a relationship, how to earn a living, and so on. Feminist counselling deals with practical issues as well as looking at unconscious motives for actions. There may be some assertiveness training, or even help with career choices or taking courses. Nothing which affects a woman's place in the present world is felt to be out of tune with feminist counselling, so the counselling sessions may cover such aspects as career, childminding, appearance, PMT and sexual harassment.

One problem with feminist counselling is that it works against the world, against the male-dominated society, and women who opt for this kind of help may well find that they no longer like the choices they made within patriarchy, such as getting married, having children, having no financial independence, but they can't always see their way clear to getting out of them. The realization that they may have been working against their own best interests may mean that their previous world is completely destroyed, but they have no other support system to put in its place. It can be extremely lonely to be a feminist and out of line with everybody else around you.

For this reason, only those women who are prepared to look at their lives very coolly, and feel really ready to make changes, should consider feminist counselling. Jocelyn Chaplin, author of *Feminist Counselling in Action*, admits that this type of therapy may be training people for a world which does not yet exist – a utopia. However, she argues, if enough women can see the point of not being hierarchical and patriarchal, then society will be changed for the better.

She believes that feminist counselling is necessarily limited in its effectiveness while we continue to have patriarchal marriages – the only type of marriage we in fact have. Until more women can see that they are doing themselves no good by perpetuating this system, then the efficacy of feminist counselling must be of limited value. It is not possible, within the parameters of feminist counselling, to be both a raised-consciousness feminist and married. The two cancel each other out – but while so many women still embrace marriage, even though by its very nature it is a relationship of inequality, then feminist counselling can only be of partial value. It is difficult, Jocelyn Chaplin says, to be healthy in an unhealthy society, and one criticism of feminist counselling is that it goes very much against our present society.

The final criticism is that, essentially, the feminist message is the same as the one seen as central by other forms of counselling, which is that you, as the client, are at least as important as anybody else, and that your views, wishes, ideas, ideals, choices and personality should be allowed to be expressed rather than crushed by other people.

New Age Counselling

This 'alternative' type of counselling does not conform to any set style but it takes its inspiration from the human potential movement of the 1960s and 1970s, and concentrates on personal growth, fulfilment of personal potential and knowing what you really want. It is useful for people who want to discover and expand their potential, rather than people who come with a specific problem, such as grief, redundancy or marriage difficulties.

It basically 'looks inward' to discover the answers and as such has been criticized for encouraging navel-gazing rather than looking outside at society's larger problems. New Age counsellors would counter this objection by saying that it is only when individuals attain awareness and think positively that society itself can be changed for the better.

New Age counselling may well involve examining attitudes to spirituality, concern for others and for the environment, and discussion as to how we can live in peace and harmony with other people and with the planet. There is not a simple New Age approach but counsellors may embrace the occult, use psychic methods, Eastern philosophies and ideas, and try to merge ancient wisdom with the way we live now.

The approach is holistic, concentrating equally on mind,

body and spirit, and helping clients to become aware of different layers of consciousness within themselves. It aims to help people contact their 'higher selves' and has as its cornerstone belief the idea that activating and understanding the Higher Self is the ultimate goal of human existence. Some New Age counsellors may also take you into past lives, with the idea that patterns of thought and behaviour going back beyond this one incarnation can be understood and brought into conscious awareness.

Although much of New Age philosophy still sounds cranky, even though it has been with us for thirty years now, it is coming ever more into the mainstream and increasingly, conventionally trained counsellors are taking at least some New Age ideas on board, even if they may not want to dabble in the occult and reincarnation. Nor do you have to personally believe in past lives or the occult to benefit from this type of counselling. As with all other styles, the proof of the pudding is in the eating and if it works, who is to ridicule it?

People often move on to New Age-type counselling after they have benefited from a more established style and feel they want to continue the personal growth they have started.

At the moment New Age counselling is rather a band wagon and anybody at all can call themselves a new age counsellor and tout for custom. There are no accredited training courses for it, and often no supervision for practising counsellors, and you may come across some therapists operating in this area who seem very weird indeed.

Counselling Workshops

Workshops – where a group of like-minded people meet to work through their problems with the help of a workshop leader – are becoming very popular indeed. They may be day or residential and are usually designed to help you work through a specific problem in the company of others who have been through similar traumas or difficulties to yourself.

The major benefit of the workshop approach is that clients feel they are not alone and that the disturbing, disgusting or inappropriate feelings they hold (according to them) are actually shared by everyone else in the workshop. Very often, this realization that the problem is a common, rather than an unusual one, forms part of the healing process.

As with so many forms of therapy these days, the workshop idea is basically American and it seems to work particularly well with people who have relationship difficulties. Through the group, and through various techniques, such as role play, role reversal and drama, hidden feelings and emotions come to the surface. An important aspect of workshops is the group support and the closeness that develops when people are working through their difficulties together.

Workshop leaders are usually trained counsellors, who may have added on the workshop idea after their basic training. Successful workshops that have been held in recent times include those called 'Women Who Love Too Much', where women who tend to form a succession of relationships with destructive men can come together and work through the reasons why they need to sabotage themselves in this way, and 'Loving Relationships Training', where people come on weekend courses to learn how to love themselves and others better.

Workshops are now being held for divorced people, who can meet for a weekend to talk through and understand their problems; for survivors of incest and child abuse; for victims of accidents; and for cancer patients. The subjects being treated by the workshop approach are expanding all the time and this style of counselling is suitable for those who feel safer, less alone and less vulnerable in a group than they might in a one-to-one situation.

Another advantage of workshops is that they tend to be

much cheaper than individual sessions, which may be one reason why they are becoming so popular.

Many of the types of counselling described above, which are outside the mainstream approach of client-centred or psychodynamic counselling, have no BAC-recognized counsellor training courses. They are considered specialist or fringe therapies. There is no doubt, however, that these different forms of counselling can often help – particularly where conventional counselling leaves a gap.

But when considering, or booking up, a form of counselling where there is no external form of accreditation, you do of course have to be even more wary. For example, there are, without doubt, fake psychics and inexpert hypnotherapists who can do more harm than good, though such people are probably more incompetent than actually setting out to do harm. Although the numbers of out and out tricksters may be small, the fact is that very many people professing to be psychic simply do not have the powers that they claim. Also, many hypnotists have set up in practice after discovering in themselves some ability to produce altered states in others – but without having had any proper training or finding supervision of their work.

If you are interested in a more 'alternative' form of counselling, the rules are simple: proceed only on recommendation from somebody that you trust and check out everything you possibly can about them. Finally, listen to your instincts and get out if you feel uneasy.

Whatever kind of counselling people go to, it is always, finally, for emotional reasons. Some may go because they feel generally unhappy and unfulfilled in their lives, but most are brought to counselling because of something quite specific, such as trying to cope with the death of someone close, redundancy, the break-up of a marriage or close relationship, sexual difficulties or a serious illness. In the next chapter, we will look at how counselling can help people with specific problems.

5

Counselling for Specific Issues

Most people only consider counselling when some serious crisis happens in their lives. Shattering events which may take people into counselling include the death of somebody close, being made redundant, or becoming seriously or terminally ill. For other people, it may be something quite small that finally pushes them to the edge – yet another row in a long-deteriorating relationship, but this time it feels like the end of the road. It is at such times that people often feel they cannot cope alone, that they cannot make sense of what is happening to them and have no idea how to continue in the face of such overwhelming feelings.

Sometimes, as with redundancy or serious illness, counselling may be provided by the company or by the hospital or hospice caring for the sick person. Indeed, with some illnesses, such as AIDS and cancer, counselling is now recognized to be an integral part of the treatment. Even, or perhaps particularly, when there is little hope of recovery, it is considered useful, for the quality of life is as important as the quantity. Where counselling is not so readily provided, it is nevertheless likely to be available for other specific issues and this chapter looks at the particular kinds of counselling on offer.

Bereavement Counselling

At some point in our lives we will all be called upon to face the death of somebody close to us – a parent, partner, sibling, friend, and for some of us even our child. Because the death of a loved one will eventually happen to us all, we will look first at bereavement counselling, which is now one of the most important areas.

The 'grief counselling' movement really started with the work of Elisabeth Kubler-Ross, whose methods and understanding of death and dying have helped very many people to come to terms with a loss of this kind. Dr Kubler-Ross described several stages of attitudes which are common when faced with death. These go from numbness and denial to accepting the reality and finally to depression. These stages happen whether the person is trying to face up to his or her own death or that of somebody close.

Of course, not everybody will go through these stages, as we are all individuals, and bereavement counsellors should not anticipate certain stages or attitudes. But, through their experience, they will – or should – be prepared for wild swings in emotions, from rage, guilt and anger to sheer disbelief and refusal to accept the reality of what has happened. These feelings are often more frightening because in our modern Western society we tend to shut off the idea of death as something almost unnatural. Few of us have seen a dead body and most of us are unprepared, and often have no religious faith to help us, when we come up against the pain and sadness of death – and the grief experienced by either ourselves or bereaved people we know.

People specialising in bereavement counselling will often, although not always, be those who have had to come to terms with death themselves and have grown stronger and more self-reliant because of it. A bereavement counsellor will understand that it can take a very long time before there is final acceptance of the reality and calmness in the face of what has happened.

Paula, whose four-year-old daughter died suddenly and without warning, was saying months after the event: 'I still believe that I will blink, and she'll be back.' She admitted that she fully expected to find her daughter in her bed in the mornings and at home when she returned from work. And this was after having extensive counselling.

But, said Paula, she does not know how she would have coped without the counselling. 'I didn't understand my feelings at all. There was a wild mix of emotions. I kept breaking down in tears at work and had the feeling that nothing mattered any more. At the same time, part of me knew that I had somehow to carry on, that being incapacitated by grief wasn't going to help anybody, least of all myself.'

The most valuable aspect of the counselling, said Paula, was that she was given permission to grieve openly. 'As a business executive, I might have tried to hide it, keep up the facade,' she said. 'But my counsellor said that it was important to grieve, to talk about my daughter, to try to accept whatever I was feeling at the time.

'The very strength of the emotions I felt was overwhelming and there were days when I felt I couldn't do anything at all, even get up. Somehow, I've managed to keep my job going and keep the house in some sort of order. I don't know when, if ever, I'll feel "normal" again – but it helped to know that what I was going through is what commonly happens when someone is faced with such a terrible event. Otherwise, I might have thought I was going mad with grief.'

When there is a bereavement, the shock is often so great that the person simply cannot take it in. The bereaved person may behave as if the deceased is merely lost and will eventually be found. The death of a child can be the hardest of all to accept, for it seems to reverse the natural order of things, whereby the older people are expected to die first. Also, children's deaths are so rare, compared to the past, that most of us are simply not prepared for such an eventuality.

Bereavement counsellors say that death hits people hardest when they have no previous experience of it – and these days, many of us will not have had direct experience.

I, for instance, have never seen or touched a dead person and since most people now die in hospital, this is the norm. Death, like many other natural functions in life, has been tidied away, sanitized, and there seems to be a conspiracy in which we all collude that it does not exist. This attitude has reached its most extreme form in America, where people can now have their bodies frozen after death, to keep them in a state of perfect preservation until a cure is found for the 'disease' that killed them off and they can be brought back to life.

In our present society, we are more afraid of death and dying than of anything else, which is why there is so much denial of the reality. Usually, strong negative emotions will accompany the denial. There will commonly be guilt and anger, rage against the doctors or nurses in hospital who failed to prevent the death, a terrible desire for revenge on the person who ran the now dead person over, or who was responsible for his or her care, in the case of an accident. The court cases often brought by parents whose children died in accidents on school ski-ing trips, for example, is one way that denial and blame commonly come in to cloud the reality of the death.

Most bereaved people cannot ever believe that life will seem normal again or that they may feel 'themselves' once more. A counsellor will be able to help the bereaved people work through their grief, offer support through all the stages and, most important of all, help them to accept the reality and finality of the death. Help may also be needed to adjust to the world outside once more, where the dead person will forever be missing.

Once the various stages of grief have been worked through, the counsellor will help the bereaved person to refocus their energies in a more positive way. Nobody can say in advance how long this process will take, as nobody knows in advance what anybody's coping mechanisms might be.

Bereavement counselling will also help where there has

been a miscarriage or stillbirth. With both, it is now understood that the process of grieving must be gone through, in order to cancel what might otherwise become an endless tape running round in the head. It is considered very important to be able to mark the loss, to accept that it has happened, which may mean arranging some kind of ceremony or ritual which signifies that the loss has occurred. Often, until there has been a ritual of some kind, there is not genuine acceptance of the loss.

Sometimes, bereavement counsellors can offer specific healing advice. Mandy, who suffered a very late miscarriage after becoming pregnant for the first time at the age of forty, was advised to plant a tree in memory of the son she never had. Now, as she watches the tree grow, she can be reminded of her loss in a positive way. 'I found this advice to be more healing than any other,' she said. 'It helped both me and my husband to accept the reality and to feel that our son was a person, not just embryonic tissue and organs.

'We had already decided on a name – we knew it was a boy because of the amniocentesis test – and our counsellor advised us always to think of him by this name. Now, we think of that tree as Stephen's tree. Some people might think it's not a good idea to be reminded of a miscarriage in this permanent way but we have found it to be extremely helpful.'

Mandy did go on to have another baby at the age of forty-two, a healthy daughter. 'But Stephen will always be a reality,' she said. 'We haven't tried to pretend that that pregnancy didn't exist, or can be discounted because we now have a lovely daughter.'

Bereavement counsellors will also understand that the loss of a close family member will inevitably put a strain on other relationships. It is not uncommon for marriages to break up under the strain of facing a child's death, and for all kinds of recriminations and problems to come out. Blame is usually uppermost: if you hadn't let him go on that trip, if you'd let her stay off school that day, if you hadn't been a working mother, if you hadn't been such an absent father . . .

With the death of elderly parents, even though the shock may not be so great, especially if they have been ill for some time, the impact can still be immense. There may be regrets that peace was never made, that so many things were left unsaid. There may also be the realization that the next generation, previously regarded as 'children', are now the true grown-ups. Many women feel that with the death of their mother, they now truly have to fend for themselves – even if they have been doing this in reality for very many years and even if the tables might have been turned, with the daughter looking after the elderly parent during her last years.

All these emotions can be made easier to handle with the help of a counsellor. She or he will also be able to help if the parent who died has not been liked, if there has not been a good relationship and if there is relief that this person is now dead – often accompanied by guilt feelings. People may not be able to accept the reality of their parents' characters or actions, so much do they want to believe their parents had their best interests at heart. Counsellors help the bereaved to come to terms with everything they might be feeling and encourage them to go through these emotions, not try to pretend they don't exist.

With the death of a spouse, there may be terror at the thought of coping on one's own. Many long-term marriages, even if they have not been happy, become over the years like entwined trees and without the other half it may feel as though there is simply no means of survival. Death hits spouses especially hard where there has been a very strong division of labour, such as where the wife has become queen of the kitchen and the domestic arrangements, and the man has dealt with all the financial aspects. Suddenly coping with all these as well as the actual death may seem too much.

Bereavement is also problematic where the relationship

has not been good, where there has been constant quarrel-
ling and bickering, or where one partner has been alcoholic, addicted to drugs or was flagrantly unfaithful. Here
again, there may be guilt and blame – and the counsellor
will help the bereaved person to work through this.

Bereavement counselling may be individual, group or
with the family – depending on the wishes of the bereaved. Most people who have had bereavement counselling feel that it has been invaluable, partly because so many
of us do not have family or local support systems any more
and realize that when something like this happens, we
simply have nobody to turn to.

In many ways, a bereavement counsellor may be better
than the family, because she or he will be detached and
objective, not caught up in the emotions, and will (or
should) offer empathy, not sympathy. A sympathetic
person may offer condolences such as: 'You must miss him
after all this time together' – telling the bereaved person
how they ought to feel. It may be the reality that the
bereaved person is glad their partner is gone but can't
bring themselves to admit this. They will be able to admit
this, or any other ambivalent feelings, to the counsellor.
Indeed, the counsellor will probably be the *only* person
such things can be admitted to.

Death, particularly after a painful illness, can often act as
a great relief – and this feeling too, needs to be acknowledged. Few of us have unambivalent feelings about those
who are close to us and counsellors can help any negative
as well as positive emotions concerning the dead person
to come to the surface and be acknowledged.

Many people find that the experience of a death can
help them to grow and change, and sort out what they
want from life. As they now have to go through the rest of
their lives without this person, whatever the quality of the
relationship, it will be a time for assessing priorities,
determining future lifestyle and becoming more clear
about what they want.

It is now also possible to go for counselling to learn how to face up to your own death. As this is the greatest fear of all, it is now recognized that counselling in advance can greatly help people. In the days when most of us believed in an after-life, perhaps death did not seem so final. But now, with our materialistic outlook, death is often seen as the ultimate insult. Doctors and hospitals have not helped here by inventing life-support machines and ways of keeping people alive for a long time when, in previous ages, they would have died. Because we believe that death is the very worst thing that can happen, we do everything in our power to prevent it happening – and then we are shattered and unable to cope when it does, inevitably, take place.

Serious Illness Counselling

Any serious illness has a profound emotional as well as physical impact. It not only brings up the prospect of death, with all the fears that that can entail, but may well have serious practical consequences for our lifestyle. We may have to face the loss of a job, of income, of physical independence; the future becomes suddenly very uncertain and frightening. People may suffer extreme mood swings from optimism to despair.

Counselling is now recognized to be of great benefit for anybody threatened by serious illness, both to help cope with the emotions involved and to provide as much information as possible about the illness itself and its likely progress – the unspoken imaginings of what may happen are often the cause of unnecessary fears. The counsellors may be people who have the illness and have come to terms with it but always they will be people who have made a close study of the emotions and problems involved. One of the first things that counsellors will point out is that any serious illness does not just affect the person but every relationship, every aspect of their life. As for other types of counselling, the most important thing will be to accept the reality of what has happened and not to deny it.

There are often national organizations, with local branches, set up to help with specific illnesses, for example, multiple sclerosis, diabetes, Alzheimer's disease, and they may be able to put you in touch with specialist counsellors. Here, we will look at the two major illnesses, AIDS and cancer, where counselling has become an integral part of the treatment.

AIDS and HIV Counselling

There are two distinct counselling aspects here. One is the kind of counselling that understands that the person is an individual facing a crisis. The other is about giving expert information on all the medical and social issues involved, the type of treatments available, support groups, the likely outcome of the disease. It should be stressed that, although much is known about AIDS, HIV and ARC (Aids-Related Complex), there is still a great deal that is not known – we are proceeding on interim information for the present. Nobody knows, for instance, exactly how many people in the world may be HIV positive, how long it will take for those now diagnosed positive to succumb to the full-blown disease, whether any more effective treatments will be devised in the meantime and whether a 'cure' may be round the corner – on present knowledge, this seems unlikely.

Counsellors must be able to give information on matters relating to jobs, insurance, travel abroad and so on. Above all, the purpose is to enable those with AIDS and HIV (there has been great objection to the term 'victim') to accept what has happened and to do their best to gain a sense of control over their illness and their lives. Counselling is aimed at reducing anxiety: it is known that immune systems are impaired by mental stress and the most important thing with HIV is to keep the immune system as strong as possible.

Counsellors will also give advice on safer sex and say what is known at present about how AIDS is spread. They should not offer moral guidance, say that homosexuality or promiscuity are wrong. Any supposed AIDS counsellor who offers moral advice or comment on past behaviour should be dismissed instantly. It is always better to gain support through a recognized AIDS support system, as these people really are the experts. Don't listen to uninformed opinion and advice; with something as devastating as AIDS, informed, impartial advice and information must always be sought.

Counselling may involve preparation for death. One of the saddest aspects of AIDS is that the people affected are often young men and women, and AIDS counsellors need to be particularly strong emotionally in order not to be overwhelmed by the decimation of life and promise.

Although AIDS is the most terrible illness of our time, there are now excellent support systems available and anybody who has reason to fear HIV should get in touch with one of these (addresses at the back of the book) without delay. They really do know how to help.

Cancer Counselling

Many research studies have now shown that counselling is of immense value with cancer. In fact, it is so much a part of cancer treatment these days that it is hard to imagine that only ten years ago, in the early 1980s, there was hardly any cancer counselling at all. The disease was still so much feared it was hidden and those who contracted any form of cancer usually suffered in silence, pretending that they had something else. Relatives and friends would similarly not admit the reality of cancer and the word was usually only spoken of in hushed tones.

Thankfully, cancer is now out into the open and it is

mainly because of the cancer counselling movement that we can now talk about the disease and lessen our fears. Writer Susan Sontag, who dismisses much of the 'alternative' healing work now going on with cancer patients, has stated that the reason cancer has come into the open is because it is no longer our most feared disease – AIDS has replaced it. Be that as it may, many cancer patients have discovered a whole new outlook on life thanks to their illness. They have realized, with the help of experienced counsellors, that facing up to their illness can actually be something positive rather than overwhelmingly negative.

As proof of the proliferation of the cancer counselling movement, there are now more than 300 self-help cancer groups in the UK, where cancer patients can come together to talk about their illness and face up to the issues involved. It is now accepted that it is far better to tell the truth to one's family and friends, on the understanding that a trouble shared is a trouble halved. Suffering in silence is never recommended. The more cancer is talked about, the more the fear recedes. Once the family can be included, they may all go for counselling, so that a healing environment can be provided, once there is understanding.

Most of people's fear lies in anticipation, rather than what is actually happening at the time. Part of the job of cancer counsellors is to explain what is likely to happen, although they should not anticipate your emotions or tell you what you ought to feel.

Counselling is of prime importance at the Bristol Cancer Help Centre, where much of the therapy concentrates on dealing with emotional pain – often worse than the physical discomfort or difficulties caused by invasive treatment. Many cancer patients feel, rightly or wrongly, that they are pushed out by their loved ones and treated differently, sometimes even excluded, as if the illness is catching. It is other people's fear that makes them behave like this.

Sometimes, according to Dr Rosy Thompson, who counsels patients at the Help Centre, relatives may behave as if the patient has died already. This tends to happen with a diagnosis of serious cancer and is the relatives' way of trying to adjust to life without this person. With understanding, they can be helped to change their approach. Rosy Thompson says that the main function of a cancer counsellor is to help patients come out of the condition of solitary confinement and put them back in touch with their feelings and also their close relatives and friends. It can, she says, be a considerable relief for patients to be able to talk to somebody who is not afraid of them and who treats them as a proper human being.

As with any other crisis, a diagnosis of cancer often forces people to re-examine their priorities and perceptions, and re-evaluate their lives. Now that such a serious issue is threatening, things which are petty or unimportant can be seen as such.

Often, cancer patients have in the past been excellent at coping. They are frequently the people who hold the household together, the ones who never complain, the ones who everybody else turns to. They also often seem extremely nice people – but underneath they may have been suppressing anger, rage, resentment. Some cancer patients strongly resist the idea that it is their personality and attitudes which have contributed to the cancer and prefer to attribute it to some outside agency, such as environmental pollution or genetic inheritance. It is important that cancer sufferers do not blame themselves for their illness – they have enough to cope with already – but cancer counsellors will aim to encourage sufferers to own their cancer and to accept that their attitudes may be contributory factors to their suffering.

In her book *Loving Medicine*, Rosy Thompson says that great personal breakthroughs often happen when cancer patients come for counselling. They can learn to be more themselves, not try to put up a coping facade all the time, and can release all their bad feelings about themselves and other people. It is the job of the counsellor to provide an environment where this kind of release will be possible. This is unlikely to occur by talking to family or friends, or even the doctor.

Cancer counsellors can also help patients to discover what they really want to do in life. Often a realization that time might be short will catapult people into living their own lives for the first time, and reconsidering priorities.

The kind of counselling used at the Bristol Cancer Help Centre is eclectic, influenced by the transpersonal movement and also by Eastern, Jungian and Freudian ideas. There is an aspect of Rogerian therapy, too, as the Centre believes that basically we are all experts on ourselves – it's just that our real 'selves' often need help to be realized.

Cancer counsellors, like others, offer unconditional positive regard, detached love and an atmosphere of acceptance. Many cancer patients, says Rosy Thompson, end up grateful to the illness for giving them a chance to look at themselves and to learn lessons about themselves that may not have happened otherwise. The illness has been a sign that our lives have gone out of balance in some way and we can get them back in balance, if we want to.

Of course, cancer counselling is not a magic cure and people who go for counselling in hopes of eliminating the cancer may be bitterly disappointed. They may find that their cancer does not improve or indeed, it may get worse and they may die. But nobody knows how long they've got and the main function of cancer counselling is to add quality to the length of time that is left.

Most cancer counselling is carried out on a group basis, although there is individual counselling as well. The idea is that through the group, people will come to see that they are not alone, that whatever doubts, fears and problems they may have will also have been experienced by others in the group. Nowadays, many people who have survived cancer become cancer counsellors, to help others to arrive at a level of peace and acceptance which they may not otherwise be able to do.

Trauma Counselling

The purpose of trauma counselling is to help people come to terms with a terrible happening in their lives. This might be a very bad accident, such as a train, car or plane crash or a natural disaster; it could be rape, incest, mugging or any other kind of violence and abuse. If the event is very recent, the counselling aims first to help the person over the immediate shock; sometimes, the event will have happened long ago and may even have been consciously forgotten for years, but is now returning to haunt the victim. In either case, post-trauma stress syndrome is now a recognized condition which, if not treated, may turn into actual mental illness. Agoraphobia, panic attacks, recurring nightmares, obsessional states, may all result from a bad trauma.

In counselling, clients will be taken gently through the event or events that have been troubling them at a very basic level and will be encouraged to go through all the emotions that they are experiencing and that they may have previously blocked off. Trauma counselling is designed to help us to remember, not to forget, so that we are no longer blocking off important memories and denying part of our experience. Until such events can be brought out into the open and their impact emotionally acknowledged, they will continue to exert their influence. Guarding a secret and suppressing fears takes up a lot of energy, which could be more usefully employed to realize potential and be more effective in the present.

People will therefore be encouraged to talk about exactly what happened to them and they may need to do this many times before the event begins to lose its power to traumatize and they can begin to sort out their emotions. With some forms of victim counselling, clients are encouraged to keep a diary where they record everything they are feeling, including emotions they are not 'supposed' to feel, such as the conviction that they 'deserved' the crime, are to blame for provoking the attacker, that they are a bad or 'marked' person. There is often a strong desire for revenge and these emotions have to be worked through along with all the others.

Most trauma counselling is done on an individual basis, although group sessions may be available as well. Counsellors require very careful training and supervision to cope themselves with the intensity of the clients' experiences. This is particularly true of counselling for incest and child abuse where sometimes the memory has been so blocked off that the person may deny that it ever happened. It is now well known that children often 'go out of themselves' when being abused, in order to survive the event. In such case, hypnotherapy is occasionally used (with of course the client's consent) to enable regression to take place. The counsellor will then ask questions, as if the client is a child. For example, the client may be asked to remember a happy day at the beach. 'What are you doing now, dear?' the counsellor may ask, to which the 'child' may reply: 'I'm playing with my bucket and spade.' The counsellor may then ask: 'Who is with you?'

By gentle questioning, counsellor and client will arrive at a time when the child is scared, when she hears Daddy coming up the stairs and is pretending to be asleep so that Daddy will not molest her. Gradually, through the questioning, the incident of abuse will come out into the open and emotions start flooding out.

The painful and usually very confused emotions connected with child abuse may take years to come to terms with, and always leave their scar, but trauma counsellors firmly believe that such deep hurts (which are of course not restricted to child abuse) can never be healed unless they have been re-experienced in the present — with a person who can provide support and understanding.

Rape Counselling

The question of what does or does not constitute rape is still being hotly debated. Some forms of rape are obvious: if a woman (or man — it is being increasingly realized that male rape is by no means as rare as once thought) is sexually assaulted by complete strangers, then there is usually no argument. But what if the alleged rapist is a husband, or partner or other close relative? What if it all happened a very long time ago?

Although there are no absolute cut and dried answers, any act of sex where there is not mutuality can be considered rape. The relationship at the time of the assault is immaterial — and most rape crisis centres acknowledge this. Rape can take place within a supposedly loving relationship — and often does.

Many people who have been raped, or forced into acts of sex, believe, however, that they are responsible for the assault and that they somehow goaded or encouraged the rapist to perform the act. Because of the guilt and blame attached, not to mention the possibility that the rapist may be the person 'who pays the rent', the supposed 'protector' of the victim, there is often great reluctance to step forward and talk about it. If the rape happened a long time ago, there may be layers of denial and repression; some people who go for therapy are surprised that a memory of rape surfaces when consciously they had forgotten all about it. It is also important to understand that rape is very common — not the rare, out of the blue act of violence it is often thought. Rape is any sexual act where somebody forces themselves on you, or tells you you mean yes when you say no.

At one time, victims were extremely reluctant to go to

the police, for fear they would be dealt with unsympa-thetically and possibly, physically harshly by the police doctor. Those days are almost over and police are now very often trained in rape counselling; victims, too, can always ask to be seen by women officers.

Rape counsellors understand the feelings the victim is going through, or may have been through, and will talk them through the assault, ask whether they want to bring charges, and tell them what their rights are. They also understand that after the experience of rape, life will never be the same again. There may be feelings of revulsion with oneself, with any kind of close relationship, there may be a shutting off from other people. Victims often feel they deserved the rape and may start sabotaging or injuring themselves afterwards.

Rape crisis centres can also help women with rehousing, social security payments, getting children looked after and other practical considerations if the rapist is a husband or partner. Advice can also be given as to how you can protect yourself in future from further attacks. Rehabili-tation and the establishment of trust may take a long time and counsellors will try to help people to see themselves as 'survivors' rather than 'victims' and aim to enable them to take charge of their lives without fear, without blame and without the huge burden of guilt. Finally, they may help clients to see that they can emerge stronger than before.

Alcohol and Drugs Counselling

There are now very many agencies for dealing with alcohol and drug problems. They range from social service and charity organizations providing free services to resi-dential drying-out and rehabilitation centres which have been called 'twice as expensive as Eton' — although not profit-making enterprises they may charge huge sums for residence and therapy.

Never imagine that a drink or drugs problem cannot be helped. The trouble is that very often, those most needing to be helped to free themselves from drink or drugs are those who do not see that they have a problem – the hold of any mood-altering substance increases along with denial.

Many agencies for alcohol and drink problems are based in the twelve-step 'Anonymous' programmes, where the first step is to admit you are powerless over the substance. 'Anonymous' organizations, started in America over fifty years ago by two alcoholics, have proved themselves consistently the most successful way of overcoming substance abuse. The alcoholic, or addict, will never say 'I *was*, but I *am* alcoholic' and will then take it 'one day at a time'.

Most, although not all, counsellors who specialize in this field – and addiction is a highly specialized area – will themselves have had substance abuse problems and will have reached their personal 'rock bottom' before they try to counsel others. Counsellors will understand that stopping drinking or taking drugs is not a simple matter of an act of will – their clients are in the grip of an addiction they have become powerless to control. Counsellors also know, often from bitter experience, that stopping any substance abuse can take years and be accompanied by a great deal of backsliding. There will also be serious withdrawal problems and these too need careful and sympathetic handling.

We are only just starting to acknowledge the toll that alcohol abuse is taking, not only on the alcoholic or active drinker, but on other members of his or her family. 'Anonymous' organizations now have support groups for relatives, where they can talk over their problems, which are often as great. It has been said that the life of an alcoholic or drug addict seriously disturbs that of at least five other people. All these may need to go for counselling as well.

Until very recently, alcohol, drugs and all mind-altering substances or activities were shrouded in a veil of secrecy. Few people admitted that they, or members of their family, had such a problem. It would be good to say that this attitude has disappeared, that everything is now out in the open. Unfortunately, this is not true and there is still great denial and shame surrounding any addiction.

It is largely because of the great shame, accompanied by ferocious denial and inability to take responsibility for one's actions ('It was a woman who drove me to drink,' said W.C. Fields and added: 'And I never had the grace to thank her') that addiction counselling is such a specialized world. It needs careful training and assessment because counsellors themselves have an uphill struggle – the addiction can prove to be stronger than either the counsellor or the client.

As active addicts are so reluctant to go for counselling or help – they cannot bear the thought of being parted from their substance, which has become their best, and often only, friend – it may be necessary for the spouse or other family member to seek help first, either from the GP or from Al-Anon or Families Anonymous, the support groups for those affected by another's substance abuse. Expert help may be necessary, because very often family members will unwittingly become 'enablers', paying bills, mopping up mess, hiding drink or drugs, or otherwise colluding in the addiction.

It is most important to seek help for any serious addiction, and particularly so where children are involved. One counsellor said: 'If I'd had a penny for every time a woman told me she'd protected her children from their alcoholic father, I'd be rich indeed. 'The only way of 'protecting' one's family is to seek help as soon as possible. Counsellors working in this field know that it is not easy and they will not sit in judgement upon somebody who cannot give up their addiction, however much it is ruining everyone's life.

It always takes courage to admit that one may need counselling but where addictions are concerned, it needs more courage than ever. It is almost impossible to withdraw from a serious or long-term addiction without skilled help, either from those further along the road of recovery, such as the 'Anonymous' organizations, or from a professional counsellor specializing in this form of help.

A list of AA, Al-Anon and Narcotics Anonymous Fellowships, and their various offshoots can be found in the local telephone directory. There is also GA and Gam-Anon for gamblers and their families.

Tranquillizer Counselling

It is only since the mid-1980s that doctors and the general public have realized that problems of drug addiction don't just apply to alcohol or heroin and other illegal drugs but also to tranquillizers and sleeping pills which were previously considered quite harmless. But it is one thing to realize their addictive qualities, and quite another to be able to withdraw successfully.

Over the past few years, a number of tranquillizer help groups have been set up, almost always by people who have managed to withdraw themselves. Joan Jerome, who set up the first of the self-help groups for tranquillizer users in the UK, says that the hell of tranquillizer withdrawal can never be overestimated. 'Speaking from experience, I would say that it's far, far worse than trying to withdraw from street drugs such as heroin. When I was in a Drug Dependency Unit in hospital, all the heroin users had withdrawn far more quickly, and with far fewer bad side-effects, than me.'

It is now well known that tranquillizers are powerful depressants and can have far-reaching effects on mental, emotional and physical health. Tranquillizer counsellors understand that, in withdrawal, there are two probelms to be overcome – that of withdrawing from the drug and that of facing up to the original reason for taking it.

Some doctors can now put people in touch with tranquillizer counsellors or work with their patients to devise a safe withdrawal plan. The pills must always be withdrawn gradually – going 'cold turkey' is emphatically not recommended – and support is needed through the emotional turmoil that follows being freed from the anaesthetic effect of the drugs. Much tranquillizer counselling is group work and provides the understanding and support of those who have been there themselves or who are in the same situation.

Couples Counselling

Couples – or marital – counselling is becoming increasingly common as ever more marriages break down and partners appear to experience difficulty in relating to each other. In order for such counselling to work, both partners have to agree that they have problems which they cannot sort out for themselves and for which they feel they need some expert help. The commonest complaint that partners bring is that the relationship would be all right if only the other would change, be more reasonable, more understanding, different.

One of the main tasks of the counsellor is to enable partners to appreciate that it is not possible ever to change the behaviour of another person. Unless that person sincerely wants to change, and is committed to doing so, then there is no room for manoeuvre. Any suggestion that the other person may change is usually met with enormous resistance. 'Why should *I* change?' the partner asks. 'You are the one who needs to change your attitudes.' Until deadlocks like this can be broken, little can be achieved.

Frequently, if one partner mentions the possibility of counselling, the other will resist the idea strongly and may actively sabotage it. This is probably a reflection of the problems in the relationship, where the individuals no longer see eye to eye. What may have seemed endearing at one time has become profoundly irritating. In growing up, partners often grow apart and usually one recognizes this while the other does not. But if one partner won't agree to counselling, it does not mean that the other cannot go to seek help alone – indeed, this is very common.

Couples counselling attempts to break down hostilities, to provide an environment where each partner can talk freely, with the counsellor acting as referee. The counsellor should not take sides but should be able to assess the situation for what it is and see the hidden agenda behind the apparent one.

Nikki, who with her now ex-husband Gerald went for couples counselling when their marriage hit severe problems, said: 'Things got so bad that in the end the only way we could communicate with each other was through the counsellor. Although the marriage broke up in the end, it was achieved with far less rancour than would have happened without counselling.'

The counsellor will try to get each partner to understand that choices have been made which seemed good at the time, but which may be no longer applicable.

Case History

Suzie suggested that she and Rob went for couples counselling when Rob decided to move from London to Hong Kong. Suzie had spent many years as a company wife and no longer wanted to play this role. She felt that over the years she had lost all sense of personal identity. Also, she had just fixed up a two-year course in interior design at a local college. To go with Rob to Hong Kong would mean uprooting the family once more and would put back her projected career – on hold anyway for many years – yet further.

She was determined not to go but Rob was as determined to make the career move. It would mean lots more money, less tax to pay, more prestige and a more exciting job than he had in London. Suzie felt that Rob was putting undue pressure on her to go with him. Not only that, but several of her women friends intimated that she ought to go, in case Rob fell in love with a local girl while he was out there. Suzie thought: I'm not going to be a prostitute to my own husband. The attitude of her woman friends angered her.

It was all very difficult and Suzie could see no solution. One day in the hairdresser's she read an article on marriage guidance and afterwards suggested that she and Rob fix up a few sessions. He was adamantly against it, saying that as far as he was concerned, the position was clear: he wanted to go to Hong Kong and he wanted Suzie to go with him. He pointed out that she had always accompanied him before – why was she changing now? He also pointed out how easy and pleasant her life would be – with servants, loads of money and plenty of freedom.

Rob had been brought up in an upper-middle class home with servants and saw himself very much as the breadwinner. His parents had both died when he was young and he had taken responsibility for his younger sister and brother.

In the end, to please Suzie, and to try to persuade her to go with him, he agreed to see a counsellor. Both Suzie and Rob were very indignant at the outset and both were determined not to shift their positions. The counsellor surprised them both by asking questions about their childhood and then what they both wanted out of life.

Rob had always thought the most important thing in life was to make lots of money but he discovered that this was really a rationalization. Deep down, he was not a domestic animal and did not really like family life. Also, he was nomadic and hated the thought of being settled for ever.

Suzie was different. She wanted a secure home base and

she did enjoy family life. She now bitterly regretted having been a passive company wife for so many years. The counsellor pointed out that she had been happy to do this at the outset; if her outlook had changed now, she could hardly blame Rob for wanting her to be what she always had been. Suzie felt that now their three children were teenagers, more uprooting at this delicate stage of their education would be a mistake. But Rob clearly could not stand being stuck in London.

Eventually, after about five sessions of couples counselling, they resolved the problem: Suzie would stay at the family house in London, while Rob went to Hong Kong. Yes, it would mean splitting the family up, would mean that the children did not have a father who was present, but it seemed the lesser of the two evils. Suzie realized, through the counselling, that if Rob wanted to have an affair while he was out there, there was little she could do about it. She could not control his behaviour and he should not try to control hers.

A year later, the compromise seems to have worked. Suzie is halfway through her course. Rob is making a success of his job in Hong Kong, and the children fly out to see him regularly. Suzie now says: 'If we hadn't gone for counselling at that point, we would have split up for sure. Now, we still have a good relationship, although it has been profoundly altered. But we have a far greater respect for each other and have learned not to try and dragoon the other person to conform to our wishes.'

The number of sessions needed will vary; commonly it is five or six. They enable each partner to explain what he or she believes the difficulties to be and for the counsellor to get to know each person in the relationship and come to some understanding of what the hidden problems, as well as the presenting ones, are.

In some cases, a contract or agreement may be entered into, where each partner agrees to abide by certain rules, such as being in at a certain time, cooking or not cooking the dinner, helping with housework, writing down what was spent, and so on. Entering into a contract often enables partners to understand the position more clearly. Finances, a potent area of disagreement, will be sorted out and if the wife is non-earning, ways found to give her more independence and autonomy within the relationship

Sometimes, couples counselling works to keep the relationship together. At other times, it helps the couple decide that the relationship is effectively over and in this case, the counsellor will try to help each partner separate with as little acrimony as possible

It often happens that one partner wants to separate while the other would prefer to keep the relationship going. When there are problems over whether to separate or not, and when each partner has a different view of the relationship, then individual counselling may be recommended.

It is also increasingly being realized that separation or divorce constitutes a loss which may be almost as serious as an actual bereavement and which may well be accompanied by similarly strong conflicting emotions. Here, the job of the counsellor will be to get each partner to accept the loss as permanent, to help them detach from the other – otherwise, negative attachment can last for years and blight future relationships.

Some divorce counsellors are now advising couples who no longer want to be together to mark the occasion of their divorce with some ritual or ceremony which helps to cut the tie to the old life and to move forward without regrets, without recriminations and without blame. Sometimes, a couple may be able to have dinner together on the occasion of their divorce. More often such amity is not possible but, each partner may have a small party or other gathering to mark that this period of one's life is over and a different life is about to begin.

One of the reasons that divorce causes such pain is

because it is unmarked by any ritual ending. Most occa-
sions considered important in life, most rites of passage,
are marked by some kind of ceremony. There are chris-
tening ceremonies, confirmation, engagement and wed-
ding celebrations, birthday celebrations, degree
celebrations, funerals – but nothing to mark the end of a
long-term relationship or marriage.

Part of the reason for this is the reluctance to accept the
reality and finality of divorce; often, one partner clings to
the hope that the relationship will be able to be re-
established, even if this is only a fantasy. Divorce counselling can often take the heat off a relationship which has
become bitter and acrimonious by enabling each partner
to let go with detachment and benevolence, instead of
bitterness and hostility

Conciliation services are now also becoming available
when separated or divorced couples cannot come to
amicable arrangements regarding children and property.
Reducing acrimony is considered particularly important
for helping children, who often suffer most from parental
break-ups; they are torn between two people, both of
whom they love but who no longer love each other, and
are often used as go-betweens and excuses for unreason-
able behaviour.

Men frequently feel that they have lost out completely
and that their ex-wives have gained everything – the
house, the car, the children, maintenance, all the furniture
and assets, while he is reduced to living in a small flat, even
while earning large sums of money. But whichever partner
sees themselves as the aggrieved one, conciliation counselling can be of help in putting things in perspective.

One divorced father of two said: 'I'm now earning more
than £50,000 a year, more than I've ever earned before,
but since my divorce, I've never been poorer. I have to pay
the mortgage on the ex-marital home, maitenance for my
children and for my ex-wife. This means I can't possibly
afford a proper home for myself. It's taken a lot of

counselling to be able to come to terms with these losses –
and yet the counsellor helped me to realize that, since the
divorce, I'm actually happier than I've ever been. Our
marriage was never a success, but I hung onto it because I
didn't want to lose all my material assets. Now that I have, I
realize that it's been a relatively small price to pay for my
freedom and happiness.

'The conciliation service I went to after the divorce was
invaluable, as at one time it looked as though I would
never see my children again, simply because my ex-wife
would not allow me near the house. But, thanks to the
counselling, we have worked out an arrangement which
allows me reasonable access – which was granted by the
courts but became problematic because of fetching and
carrying and differences of opinion as to how much
freedom our teenage daughters should be allowed.

'Now, at least we're on speaking terms, although
whether we'll ever become exactly friendly, I can't say at
the moment.'

Few people who get divorced finally really regret it, as
recent research shows. But it may take time to detach and
to see the relationship in a new perspective. It often
happens that we go into relationships for extremely
dubious reasons. We may imagine we are in love or that
we have made a proper choice but in fact this may not be
the case. We may have married on the rebound, because
we felt it was time we 'settled down', because we were
pregnant, because parents pressured us into it, because we
were afraid of living on our own, because we wanted
security or money – all negative reasons which have been
rationalized over the years. Counselling can very much
help individuals to see their relationship in a clearer light
but, as always, only if they are prepared to look at
themselves.

Family Counselling

This is for members of the whole family, often when there has been a problem, such as drug abuse or alcoholism. Family counselling enables each member to see how they might have been colluding in or contributing to the problem and helps them to work out strategies for the future. All the members are encouraged to see that no problem is ever isolated but something to which every member has been contributing.

In recent years there has been a lot of emphasis on healthy and unhealthy families and the differences between the two. Unhealthy families are 'enmeshed' ones, where members cannot see themselves as separate individuals. It often happens that similar problems, such as alcoholism, go down the generations and people will unconsciously seek out others with similar problem histories.

All kinds of problems may call for family counselling – debt and redundancy, separation and divorce, the death of a close family member, the disruptive or criminal behaviour of an adolescent child. It can also be of help where there has been child abuse or incest and severe relational problems such as wife battering or other forms of ill-treatment. Families rarely consider counselling until the presenting problem has become so bad that something must be done – and often they will be referred for counselling rather than initiate it themselves.

Sometimes it may be recommended *after* a drink or drug problem has apparently been overcome. Families often believe that all their problems will be over if only the using member stops using. By contrast, they often find that the recovery actually points up greater problems. While attention has been focused on the family member who drinks or uses, other problems may have been forgotten or submerged, only to come to the surface when the drink or drugs are no longer the main issue.

It may be, for instance, that the husband is recovering from a severe drink problem and is becoming 'himself' again after years of hitting the bottle. His wife may have (unconsciously) married him *because* he had a drink problem – although she will usually deny this. His drinking problem will give her a measure of control and enable her to be 'saintly' in contrast with his 'sinner' behaviour. Problems arise after substance abuse because each family member has to learn to relate to others in a new way, that is, without the drink problem being there.

Or it may be that the wife has suffered from a severe tranquillizer problem, now under control. For years, the man has been in charge because his wife was so often ill and incapable of running the household. Now, free from the pills, she has become stronger and more self-sufficient, and he has to adjust to an equal partnership, rather than one of coper and invalid.

During family counselling, many unpleasant or painful issues are likely to come up and the counsellor will try to help the family to find more functional ways of relating to each other, to get members to see that they are all linked up in some way with the problem and can never change the behaviour of another member, only their own. Once one family member manages to improve behaviour, then it often happens that all the other members will improve as well.

The hoped-for outcome is for each family member to become more detached and self-sufficient, to have more respect both for themselves and other family members, so that the whole family is able to live together more effectively. When a family has been relating in an unhealthy way for years, it takes a lot of work and effort on the part of everybody to become functional once more and nobody can expect a smooth upward path of recovery. The adult members may have to accept the painful reality of their own childhood experience and be helped not to deny or minimize this. Many people want to believe that their own parents were caring and did the right thing by them but the truth may be very far from this fantasy picture.

Counselling for Sexual Problems

Since the 'swinging sixties' people have become more aware and more open about their sexual lives and problems. Few people find that their sex lives are plain sailing but how far this constitutes a problem is for the individual to determine. Sexual counselling is usually only considered when a sexual problem becomes the focus of all difficulties in a relationship – perhaps one partner wants sex more than the other and sex becomes a bitter battlegound, or there may be a specific difficulty such as impotence, premature ejaculation, frigidity, vaginismus or dyspareunia (difficulty of intercourse) or a sexual fetish.

The first job of a sex counsellor will be to establish whether there is any physical cause for the problem. For instance, dyspareunia may be caused by a disease such as endometriosis, a painful and debilitating condition whereby little bits of endometrium (the lining of the womb) are found outside the womb, causing infertility and a number of distressing symptoms. Impotence could be a side-effect of a commonly prescribed drug, such as beta-blockers, and also of diabetes.

If no physical problem can be found, or is not relevant, the sex counsellor will try to discover what other reasons there may be for the difficulty. Sometimes sex therapists work with individuals, sometimes with couples, depending on the situation.

Sex therapy is rarely a simple matter of getting couples back to having intercourse again. The sexual problems between them could be a sign that the relationship is over or that it needs to be re-established along different lines. There could be hidden or unacknowledged homosexuality, there could be a mistress or lover in the background. The sexual relationship may be affected by a whole range of stresses, at work or home. A woman may say she has simply gone off sex, is no longer (if she ever was) turned on by her partner, and behind this there may be a long and complex history.

Sex counsellors will try sympathetically to explore exactly what are their clients' attitudes to sex, and work with this. There should be no moralizing, no attempts made to get people to enjoy sex when they don't feel inclined. Often partners cannot perform with each other because over the years they have become bored, although they can be turned on with a new partner. Some sex therapists use surrogates to re-activate libido but this remains a controversial area.

Some use a technique developed by the famous sex therapists Masters and Johnson called sensate focus, which attempts to turn bored couples back onto each other again. With sensate focus, partners lovingly explore each other's bodies but sexual intercourse is forbidden, thus taking away any performance anxiety. Overtly sexual areas, such as genitals and breasts, have to be avoided during this phase. Sensate focus is sometimes used by Relate (marriage guidance) counsellors and many couples profess to find it a wonderful relief after being expected to perform and failing to do so.

Sex is an area notorious for people not telling the truth and most sex counsellors say that what people tell them on their own is very different from what they hear when couples come together.

During the sessions, clients will be asked to examine closely all their attitudes to sex – to intercourse, to oral sex, to other activities connected with sex. Through this, they should arrive at their own conclusions and also decide whether or not they want to continue a sexual relationship with their present partner or, indeed, anybody at all.

At one time, women (and men) who did not enjoy sex

were thought to be repressed. Everybody was supposed to want sex and if you didn't, there was something wrong with you. This idea is now fallng into disrepute as we are learning that people can be as individual in their sexual appetites as in anything else and there is no reason why we should all have to conform.

For some people, sex can become an addiction and the need to satisfy sexual urges can have as powerful and destructive a hold as alcoholism or drug abuse. Sexaholics, or sex addicts, are using sex as their fix and as time goes on, they may not be able to control the addiction. Sex therapy can help in dealing with such a problem and looking at the feelings underlying the behaviour.

As with other forms of counselling, going for sex therapy can be a way of getting to know yourself better and leading a more fulfilled life in general. You need to be careful, though, that your counsellor is somebody sympathetic to your ideas and needs, and who will not try to urge you into sexual acts against your will. Note that sex counsellors should never, under any circumstances, persuade their clients into taking part in sexual acts with them. This does not ever constitute part of the treatment.

Homosexual Counselling

Even nowadays, when homosexuality is much more out in the open than before, the subject is surrounded by prejudice and bigotry, and homophobia is rife. People who are or suspect they may be gay or lesbian therefore may feel that they want counselling from people who are themselves homosexual and have personally faced the difficulties involved. No counsellor in these areas should ever try to persuade you to try to become heterosexual or attempt to 'cure' you. It is now understood that homosexuality is not something to be 'treated' but something to come to terms with. Counsellors can help gay and lesbian people – who often feel that nobody understands – to realize that they are not alone, that there is nothing wrong with feeling as they do and that there is no therapy on earth which will enable them to become 'normal'.

Modern gay and lesbian counselling does not see homosexuality as abnormal but accepts that we do not all have the same sexual orientation. Some people may be bisexual, others completely homosexual. Counsellors can help gay and lesbian people to 'come out' if that is what they finally choose to do and give support in such matters as telling parents loved ones, and coping with prejudice and possible ostracization at work or in social life. Because the counsellors are, with few exceptions, themselves gay or lesbian, they should intimately understand the issues involved.

For most gays and lesbians, the worst aspect is trying to deal with other people's prejudice. Counsellors will help confused people to understand that bigotry comes from fear and is rife everywhere. When two lesbians were brave enough to go on television and declare their love for each other, members of the studio audience cried out to them: 'Why do you have to look like men?' 'I thought you were a man', and so on. Such blind responses are commonplace.

Even at the end of the twentieth century, it is not easy to be gay or lesbian. There is a feeling in society that such people are deliberately not conforming, that they could be heterosexual if they wanted to. In fact, we know that sexual orientation is not consciously chosen – something a sympathetic counsellor will make clear early on in the sessions.

Counselling can be extremely helpful, particularly for young gay and lesbian people, who often feel desperately alone in an overwhelmingly heterosexual world, and for those who feel they are living a lie, perhaps in a heterosexual relationship, or whose religious faith seems to condemn them for their homosexuality.

Student and Youth Counselling

Most universities and large colleges now have a student counselling service to help with the many problems that young people may encounter – exam nerves, relationship difficulties, housing problems, course and career choices, for example. Students and other young people are increasingly seeking counselling, perhaps after it has been recommended by a tutor or other adult, and it can be of great benefit at a time when the individual may feel particularly confused and helpless in facing a larger world, often living away from home for the first time.

As with other forms of counselling, the whole area is more complex than may appear at first. Ellen Noonan, the author of a book on how to counsel young people successfully, says that young people have to realize that the particular problem for which they are seeking help may unconsciously have been chosen by them. It is not always a simple matter of changing the subject being studied or finding more suitable accommodation.

Counsellors specializing in helping young people will encourage their clients to look at patterns in their lives and examine their relationships with their parents, to see what can be done to restore freedom and control when the client feels caught up in a chain of circumstances apparently beyond control. Many young people are struggling to find their feet. They do not know who they really are – they manifest a 'false self', a phrase used by Winnicott – where outwardly they are coping and in control but when a crisis occurs, the brittle coping mechanisms fall apart.

As Ellen Noonan says, the question of personal identity is crucial to young people and one job of the counsellor is to help them find what their real identity is. Children are often required to play parts in the family from their earliest years. Thus, one child might be designated the 'clever' one, another the 'tomboy', another the 'clown', another the 'scapegoat'. There may be a favourite child and a less favoured one; children may exist more for the sake of the parents than the other way round. They are never allowed to be themselves. When such children move from home and these parentally imposed roles are taken away from them for the first time, they may have very few coping skills; they simply don't know how to be themselves.

Sometimes, students or other young people may seek help for problems rooted in childhood, such as stammering, bed-wetting and (increasingly) sexual abuse. The job of the counsellor may be to help the client face bad or unhelpful memories from the past and replace these with hope for the future. The essence of counselling young people is to help them move forward without the burdens of the past restricting their lives.

Many young people expect, even more than adults, that their problems will be overcome simply and quickly once they decide to go for counselling. But any kind of change and growth is rarely simple and will involve looking at uncomfortable aspects of oneself. As with other counselling, the aim is to help the client acknowledge split-off or denied parts of the self and integrate them into a more harmonious whole. This process may take many months and be characterized by many stops and starts but counsellors in this field often find their work particularly rewarding because young people can frequently adapt and change more quickly than older people and be set on a firmer course for the whole of their adult lives.

Redundancy Counselling

This is becoming increasingly important as people are laid off, sometimes at a minute's notice. At one time, many jobs were considered relatively safe but nowadays nothing is safe and many companies which mushroomed into multinational concerns are going bust overnight, with losses of thousands of jobs – and sometimes people's life savings.

Takeover bids, 'rationalization', falling export markets, bankruptcy, losses caused by cut-throat competition and undercutting of markets, amalgamation, and all the other aspects of modern business life, mean that the old idea of 'jobs for life' can no longer be considered valid. There is no guaranteed security, no old-fashioned reliable loyalty, no margin to keep employing people who are not contributing to company profits. In recent years, we have seen this lay-off policy happen in many jobs where at one time it would have been unthinkable, such as teaching.

So how do people cope with redundancy, once considered a terrible stigma and now increasingly an aspect of everyday life? One answer is with redundancy counselling, which started life in the early 1970s when the present redundancy policies first began to affect large numbers of workers. Increasingly, redundancy counselling is provided by large firms, in an attempt to 'humanize' the brutality of redundancy policies, and specific 'redundancy counsellors' have come into being.

One of the worst aspects of being made redundant is the feeling of being a victim, of helplessness. There is also almost always the worry of how financial commitments are going to be met. Most of us these days live on credit and borrowing, so that we live at a higher level than our earnings. Redundancy may mean inability to pay the mortgage – especially with interest rates fluctuating – and having to lose our house. There is also loss of status, as increasingly people's status is seen to be bound up with their job or profession, and a feeling of being put on the scrapheap. In fact, fear of redundancy is now so great that people will stay in unfulfilling and low-paid jobs simply because they seem safe.

It is the job of a redundancy counsellor to cover all

the practical questions as well as emotional aspects: finances, health, family relationships and responsibilities, relocation, leisure, age, etc.

The right kind of redundancy counselling can be extremely useful in facing both the practical and emotional difficulties but be aware that there are now people setting themselves up as redundancy counsellors who take large sums of money off you – possibly a chunk of your redundancy money – in exchange for advice that may be very dubious. Think very seriously before laying out hundreds of pounds on private redundancy counselling. If your firms does not provide it, try to go on recommendation. Or fix up sessions with a general counsellor. All properly trained counsellors will be able to handle redundancy, as this comes into what counselling is all about – change and loss. Counsellors should appreciate the complicated range of emotions facing people when they are made redundant and encourage them to work through them.

Case History

Martin was suddenly made redundant from his management job during a 'night of the long envelopes', when 300 workers were laid off. As such, there should not have been undue shame attached to this but Martin felt very betrayed and angered that this firm, where he had worked since his early twenties, could lay him off with such scant ceremony. The redundancy settlement would not keep him in the kind of life that he had become accustomed to and, at fifty-two, he felt he had little chance of finding a comparable job.

His firm was offering redundancy counselling but Martin felt this was patronizing, a sop, and decided not to go. He could not bring himself to tell his wife he had been made redundant and every morning he set off for 'work' as usual, carrying his briefcase and wearing a suit. But Martin's wife, a nurse, was not stupid. One day, after Martin had gone to 'work' as usual, she opened an envelope from his firm – because she feared the worst – and confronted Martin when he came home that night.

At first, he denied it but then admitted it and broke down, saying he had no idea how they were going to manage. Suzie was his second wife and they had two children of ten and eight. 'Would you consider going for counselling?' Suzie asked, and told him that a woman she used to work with in hospital who lived nearby had recently set herself up as a private counsellor.

Martin reluctantly agreed. He said: 'At first, I hated the sessions. I had been brought up to keep my problems to myself, and also found it extremely difficult to talk about what I was feeling.

'I had five sessions altogether and we talked about what I really wanted out of life. I had no idea – I had assumed that my job was the right one for me. But through talking, I wondered if there was something else I could do.

'I have always been interested in computers and understand them where other people often can't. The counsellor suggested that I might consider setting myself up as a private computer expert, going to firms and private people, talking them through their computer problems.

'Something clicked when we discussed that and I realized that in fact I had never really liked my job or approved of the methods of the management. I used my redundancy money to set myself up, advertise locally, and work started to come in.

'Now, I'm doing what I find really fulfilling and for the first time in my life, am actually enjoying my work.'

The specialist counselling services described above are by no means the only ones. There is now a huge range of self-help groups and counselling services for specific issues, ranging from the large and professionally organized, with head offices and dozens of paid staff, to the small and extremely local. (The sources at the back of the book list various of these.) The thing to realize is that you do not have to manage on your own – always ask your GP, health visitor, social worker, about groups in your area which may specialize in dealing with your problem.

Not everybody of course needs counselling. Although the right kind of advice and help can enable clarification of difficult issues, it should certainly not be assumed that people cannot cope on their own and need to be referred to a counsellor whenever life gets difficult. Ideally, the motivation for counselling should come from the client, not from outside agents.

The proliferation of counselling and the numerous groups and agencies offering help with particular kinds of problems may also obscure the fact that counsellors come in various guises. Self-help groups, by their very nature, are not about professional counselling and although counsellors practising in the various specialist areas will – or certainly should – have been specifically trained for the role, probably only a minority will have undergone the kind of rigorous counsellor training course that the British Association for Counselling is now calling for.

This is not to say you can't have full confidence in a counsellor who has not been through an accredited course of training. Counsellors working in specialist areas often have many years of experience, they may well have personally undergone similar ordeals and they will usually be taking their work to supervision. It is, however, worth knowing what does go into the training of counsellors in order for them to deal with the very serious problems that their clients may bring to them and in the next chapter we will look at counsellor training so that you can know what fully professional counsellors are in fact about.

6

What Makes a Good Counsellor

Although it is quite legal for anybody to practise as a counsellor without any formal training whatever, there have been increasing moves in recent years to put counselling on a proper professional footing. The British Association for Counselling, the main supervisory body in the UK, was set up in 1977 to promote awareness of the idea of counselling and raise standards of counsellor training and practice. Besides its journal and numerous counselling guides, the BAC publishes a Code of Ethics to which its members – now over 7000 – agree to abide and which therefore provides some protection for clients, who can appeal to the BAC if they think a counsellor has acted unethically – asssuming, that is, that the counsellor is a member of the BAC. Many counsellors are not, which does not of course mean they are unethical but does mean you will have little or no recourse for complaint if something goes wrong.

Many people become counsellors because they have personally been through an emotional ordeal and feel a need to help others going through similar circumstances. Others may feel that they have a flair for understanding and empathizing with other people and wish to put this to use, rather as somebody with a flair for playing the piano may want to become a professional pianist. This is where training comes in, for it is increasingly recognised that without full training and ongoing monitoring of themselves and their work, counsellors, however well motivated, may do more harm than good. Since 1985, the BAC has been looking at training courses and accrediting only those which meet certain standards. It also has introduced a system of accreditation for individual counsellors, who may not necessarily have completed an accredited course but who can show that they meet the BAC's standard of practice.

The BAC's director, Judith Baron, who has herself been a counsellor for very many years, specializing in infertility problems, says: 'When I began my career as a social worker nearly twenty-five years ago, there were no training courses at all for counsellors.

'Although counselling as a skill and profession goes back thousands of years, it is only since the mid-1960s that it has become recognized as a genuine career in its own right.'

The BAC was founded, she says, from an awareness that counselling was open to abuse and that there should be genuine standards and codes of practice. 'It was felt that there should be a yardstick to measure the kind of help that was being offered. And although anybody can still put up a plate outside their door offering counselling or psychotherapy, prospective clients can now check with us to see whether they are members.

'If they're not, and the person has not been recommended, then there should be a level of wariness. No reputable counsellor will mind answering questions about training and membership of professional bodies. Also, members of the public can bring complaints about individual members.'

The BAC's system of accreditation, Judith Baron adds, is a way that counsellors can measure themselves against extremely high standards. 'Becoming a counsellor means that you must put yourself under scrutiny, be prepared to have continuing supervision.

'One of the reasons the BAC came into existence was the realization that, in the wrong hands, counselling could do far more harm than good. If the counsellor imposed her own ideas on the client, told him what to do, attempted to advise or interfere, then it is unlikely the sessions would be very helpful.

'There is clearly a great deal of scope for the abuse of power and we try to make sure that people come to no harm. That's why the question of supervision is so important and continues to be vital for the whole of a counsellor's career.'

Because a counsellor has not been on an accredited training course, or does not have individual accreditation, does not mean that a course is no good or that such counsellors do not know what they are doing. But there are now so many weekend and short courses offered by people who themselves have been through no standard form of training, it's as well to be on your guard. You can find out whether a potential counsellor has been through a recognized course of training, or is individually accredited or is a member of the BAC (which in itself does not mean accreditation) by contacting the BAC.

In case you are wondering what all the fuss is about, counsellors are dealing with sensitive issues and often raw emotions, with an individual's personal world which is never to be entered into lightly, and you as the client are entitled to be in as safe hands as possible. In the following text we will look at the standards of counselling training and practice now considered necessary, from which you should gain a better picture of what qualifications and qualities to look for when going to a counsellor.

Training and Supervision

The idea that counsellors are well-meaning but rather bumbling and ineffectual do-gooders dies hard. It takes a lot of hard work, a lot of looking at oneself, a lot of facing of painful realities, to become a good counsellor. And the self-examination does not stop with training but is, or should be, a continuous process throughout practice.

Although possession of a certificate for qualifying from an accredited counselling course does not mean that a counsellor can be guaranteed to help you, it does indicate a level of seriousness about practising. The accredited courses are long and in some cases expensive; grants are rarely available and training may mean giving up a full-time job and will certainly entail a sacrifice of time as well as money. Courses usually last two or three years, sometimes longer, and are mainly part-time – many counsellors also work in other fields. Trainees are often required to be in therapy themselves for the whole of that time, which again can be very expensive. At the least, all of this requires a high level of commitment.

All training courses worthy of the name involve long hours of self-exploration and supervision. In addition, trainees will learn the theoretical basis for the counselling skills they are acquiring. Empathy, understanding and unconditional positive acceptance are all qualities which can, if not exactly be taught, certainly be brought out in a therapeutic context.

Trainees may also learn how to counsel in specific areas, such as marriage guidance (now increasingly known as 'relationship guidance', since marriage is now recognized not to constitute the only type of moderately permanent one-to-one relationship), bereavement or youth counselling. Sometimes, there may be an opportunity to specialize in a certain type of counselling, say in stress management.

Courses will usually involve a close look at different styles and schools of counselling and will put the whole movement into its historical context. Training is a mixture of theoretical knowledge, – there will probably be essays and projects to complete – and practical skills, with emphasis on self-analysis and clinical work with clients.

Learning to be a counsellor is not the same as learning to be a doctor or even a psychiatrist, where the training is almost entirely academic and you do not have to look at your own emotions and attitudes. In counselling courses, the most important aspect will be the ability to relate to the client, to understand his or her problems without getting personally involved in them, to be both loving and detached. Unless these qualities are present, or come out during training, there is no hope that the trainee will ever become an effective counsellor.

Training involves a large amount of self-exploration, because 'an unaware counsellor leading an unexamined life is likely to be a liability rather than an asset', in the words of Windy Dryden, author of many books on counselling. It is now known that if the counsellor becomes emotionally and personally involved in the client's problems, then the outcome is likely to be negative and may even be actually harmful. Hence, not only training but supervision is considered very important.

The self-examination required of counsellors is likely to be painful and disturbing. Many trainees are likely to have periods of doubt and bewilderment; some may even decide they do not wish to continue. Their personal relationships are likely to come under scrutiny and have to be reassessed, as well as their own childhoods and attitudes. All would-be counsellors have not only to understand the nature of transference, counter-transference and resistance, they have to experience them. It is not enough just to read about them in books.

Counsellor Jenny Bateman, who counsels management staff in industry and is also a tutor on training courses, says: 'In order to be a good counsellor, you have to have an open mind and also be prepared to be in therapy yourself.

'The importance of having been through personal therapy came home to me when I was helping a client deal with a recent loss at the same time as a close friend of mine was dying.

'I don't feel that training alone can make a good counsellor – you have to be the "counsellor" type – but certainly, it's dangerous to embark on seeing clients without having training, as you have to be prepared to look inwards.'

Jenny became a professional counsellor via a popular route. 'I was in social work for very many years, and then was attached to schools as a school counsellor,' she said.

'I trained at West Sussex in their Higher Education department, and had an extensive three-year training. After completing the training, I worked in schools and in social work, and set up on my own in 1989.

'I am doing ongoing training and supervision, and all the counselling I do is supervised. To me, this is vital.'

Jenny feels there are many potential pitfalls to becoming a counsellor. 'Sometimes you have to take risks and go with your gut reaction. You have to feel when the client is ready for confrontation, and you have to look for the patterns in their lives.

'It's important to guard against the client becoming dependent on you, and never letting you go. As a counsellor, you can start to feel very powerful, and I know there have been times when I've encouraged people to come back when I really ought to be helping them to become independent and not to need me any more.

'Parting, ending the sessions for good, can be painful both for you and for the client, but dependency must never be encouraged. You also have to be extremely careful not to be judgmental, or impose your own wishes on the client.

'When I was trying to help that client cope with a loss, I was in danger of becoming over-involved, as I identified with her feelings so strongly. This is why continual supervision is so important – it enables you to stand back and become detached so that you are not too involved with your client's problems.

'If ever I work with somebody who has been abused by a man, I'm in danger of becoming angry, so I make sure my own supervision follows directly on from a session of this kind.

'It's important to debrief, so that you can let go of that particular case and not let it run round in your head for ever.'

Because counsellors are dealing with so many difficult issues, it's important that they look after themselves, says Jenny. 'Otherwise you are in danger of suffering from therapists' burn-out, which means you are no good to anybody. It can be hard on your own personal relationships, as you very much have to keep your private and professional worlds separate, and never break confidences.'

The importance of having regular supervision came home to Louise, a marriage guidance counsellor, when she was seeing a client who was obsessed with a woman he had met briefly and could not get her out of his mind. He was terrified that this obsession was going to ruin his marriage.

Louise said: 'It brought back to me a horrible time when my own husband had a similar obsession. I'd blocked it out for many years and had completely forgotten about it until this client reminded me, with his own story.

'As he talked, all I could think about was this terrible time. In the end, I felt that, rather than being a counsellor, I needed counselling myself.'

She added: 'When you are recruited as a marriage guidance counsellor, you are warned that the training might be detrimental to you and your family. You are told that you will be different, and that everybody around you will notice the difference.

'I began my training perfectly confident that I had sorted out my own problem long ago. But eventually I felt I couldn't go on and had to have help. It took tremendous courage to confess my problem to my supervisor, as I felt very much that I ought to be able to cope, having been through so much training.'

Relate does not insist, as some organizations do, that all counsellors are in therapy themselves, although there is continual supervision. But in this instance, Louise's supervisor felt that she needed some private counselling of a type which was not available within the organization.

As the incident happened before Louise had completed her training, it made her wonder whether she was doing the right thing. 'It meant that I had to suspend my own training for six months, before I felt ready to continue.'

Zelda West-Meads, spokeswoman for Relate, says: 'During training, we make potential counsellors look at their own childhood, adolescence, hang-ups and prejudices, and become aware of these.

'A very important part of the training is to enable the counsellor to get in touch with his or her own problems. All counsellors must have a supervisor, who will sit in on cases during training, and there are also fortnightly groups where clients' cases are discussed in confidence.

'Whenever a counsellor is having difficulty with a particular case, one of the first questions that is asked is: why? Very often, it is something in their own background that is causing the block.'

The question of supervision, of continuous monitoring for those who are helping others, is only now beginning to become important. For many years, it was assumed that 'carers' would know how to manage their own lives. Now, it is understood that even the best counsellors are fallible, human and make mistakes. They need to be able to turn to somebody who can understand the personal problems a counsellor may be facing when trying to help clients.

Counselling Courses

There are now numerous counselling courses on offer, sometimes lasting a weekend or perhaps an evening a week over a period of a few months. Some may concentrate on a particular aspect of counselling, such as bereavement or stress management, and many of them (though by no means all) are very good. However, what we are considering here are the kind of qualifying courses now being recognized by the BAC and which are your best safeguard as a client, particularly if you are considering going to a counsellor in private practice. These training courses are designed to ensure that practising counsellors all know what they are doing and will be more likely to offer genuine help than to perpetrate harm.

Rigorous general counselling courses are at least one year full time or two years part time and have a high ratio of staff to students. Candidates will have to satisfy the selection panel that they have gained a degree of self-awareness and can complete the course without becoming disturbed themselves. They usually need to show evidence of some kind of helping activity, whether voluntary or paid, where empathy is of particular value. Prison visiting, for instance, might well come into this category. Formal academic qualifications are less important than personal qualities, although since the course will include writing essays or theoretical papers, candidates will probably be expected to have reached a certain educational level.

The University of Kent, which has one of the longest-established counselling courses in Britain, admitted its first students as long ago as 1964, when the term 'counselling' was hardly in common parlance. It is a two-year part-time course aimed at those already in some kind of helping profession and takes students aged over twenty-three. Although educational background and professional qualifications are taken into account when assessing potential trainees, the University's brochure stresses that the most important 'qualifications' are the requisite human qualities of empathy, understanding, open-mindedness and compassion. The University also holds series of short courses, in subjects such as marital counselling, sexual problems, bereavement and loss, and group leadership.

Kent is only one of several universities and colleges now offering a diploma in counselling skills recognized as a professional qualification by the BAC. Some other accredited courses in the UK include: the Training Course in Person-Centred Counselling and Psychotherapy, organized by the Facilitator Development Institute; the

University of London MsC in Counselling, held at Gold-smith's College; and the professional training courses in counselling and psychotherapy organized by the Psycho-synthesis Education Trust. This is to name only a few. Moreover, the BAC's system of accreditation is still only beginning (nor is it the only one – the British Psychological Society, for example, recognizes courses) and serious training courses, particularly in smaller institutes, may not yet be recognized because the procedures for recognition have still to be completed.

The Westminster Pastoral Foundation (WPF) has what has probably become one of the most comprehensive training programmes in the whole field of counselling, world-wide. Operating from headquarters in Kensington, West London, it offers a total of nine different types of courses, from a short-course programme to a diploma course in Advanced Psychodynamic Training. Its courses are recognized by the BAC and are supported by the DSS.

The WPF adheres broadly to the psychodynamic school and though originally a Christian foundation, it does not adhere to any particular religious doctrine and does not teach Christian values as part of its counselling pro-gramme. Like all other counsellors, WPF-trained counsellors are supposed to be objective, detached, non-judgmental and offer unconditional positive regard.

Some of the courses are for complete beginners, while others are designed for those who are already using some kind of counselling in their work, for example, probation officers or social workers, and who feel the need to put their counselling skills on a more professional footing. The Certificate Course in Counselling Skills and Attitudes, for example, is a part-time two-year course designed for those who already have some experience of counselling but who may not have undertaken formal training. Places for these courses are heavily over-subscribed as, indeed, they are for all reputable counselling courses these days.

Those who intend to make counselling a career in itself

usually take the Diploma Course, a professional qualification that takes two years full time, three years part time or four years on day release. The Diploma Course is very tough. Those selected will already have had some experience of counselling and must have completed a basic counselling skills course. Applicants must be aged under sixty and over twenty-five (those under this age are not usually considered suitable on the grounds that they are unlikely to have had enough experience of life).

They must also be in personal therapy and, if accepted, continue in therapy throughout the course.

The WPF also offers numerous short courses, refresher courses and introductory courses for people at various stages of being or becoming counsellors. At the moment, over 500 people go every week to the Kensington or Chelsea offices to train as counsellors and around 1000 a year book up the short courses.

Over 600 clients a week come for counselling for such problems as loneliness, depression, a major life change or crisis, marital or relationship problems, stress at work or serious physical illness. Counselling services are not free, but the organization is non profit-making and clients pay according to their means.

The Rev Derek Blows, a Jungian-trained analyst who is also a Christian minister, explained the purpose of training at the WPF:

'Anybody wishing to book up a WPF training course has to be prepared to undergo personal therapy, on the grounds that we cannot ever know what other people are going through unless we have insights into ourselves. Nobody can, of course, have been through every single experience that clients might bring to counselling, but they will be able to have a clear idea of how the client is likely to feel and respond.

'The most important thing anybody brings to counselling is themselves – the self is the instrument that counsellors use. Unless they are properly trained, though, they may unconsciously collude with the client instead of helping him.

'Counsellors have to be well enough trained to enter another person's hell, to have empathy, and to be able to cope when rage or envy may be directed personally at the counsellor. Whatever happens, the counsellor has to be able to retain her own sanity and objectivity – and achieving this takes a lot of training and effort.'

By far the most important aspect of training is the personal therapy and supervision, said Derek Blows. 'We find that during training, counsellors themselves change quite a lot. They find that problems crop up they never even knew about, so often they discover they need more time to work on themselves than they previously thought.

'Many trainee counsellors come for our courses believing they have already done a great deal of work on themselves and then find that they've hardly scratched the surface.'

Derek Blows believes that the counselling movement is going to get ever bigger, which is why proper training becomes ever more important. Nowadays, people want to have counselling rather than pills from the doctor, counselling rather than psychiatry, counselling rather than trying to put up with a bad situation on their own.

He said: 'We're living in an age where people need solutions. There is more disillusionment than ever before with external solutions to problems. We don't believe in pills so much these days, we no longer are able to take any notice of politicians, and those who are supposed to be loved ones may actually be sabotaging us rather than acting supportively. More than ever before, we have to be able to rely on ourselves, to take responsibility for ourselves, to be able to say: the buck stops here, and be our own experts on ourselves.

'We now have a great distrust of and scepticism about those in authority and are no longer prepared to take so much notice of them. That's why we need counselling so much – but it's such a responsible job that nobody should set up as a professional counsellor lightly.

'Anybody wishing to be a counsellor has to find and access internal strengths before purporting to advise others. Through counselling, and through our training courses, people can find that they have far more in common than they previously thought. Counselling can bring us all together, make us realize we are all members of a large family.

'But that can't happen without training. It's not enough to want to help one's fellow creatures – we may be bringing all kinds of personal dysfunctions to the situation and end up doing far more harm than good.'

Counsellors' Motivations

The idea of becoming a counsellor appeals to many people. It has even been said that counselling is now so popular that before long we'll all be counselling each other.

But what motivates people to undergo the long, usually expensive training courses, where they will have to come to terms with themselves, face aspects of themselves that may previously have been hidden, all in return for the privilege of practising a profession that is not well paid, or sometimes not paid at all, and which may cause emotional problems for years afterwards?

Although a few counsellors in private practice may earn large sums of money, the great majority earn either only a modest amount or sometimes nothing at all. Many counsellors work part-time, working in other capacities the remainder of the time, and many may be unpaid voluntary workers, for example, Relate marriage guidance counsellors are all unpaid, though they have to undergo proper training as well as being in continual supervision.

Clearly, it's not the money. Is it the power? Is it altruism, the wish to help? Is Jeffrey Masson right when he says in

Against Therapy that all therapists eventually become corrupted? Or is the gentleman just protesting too much, after his own disillusionment with therapy became profound?

In his book *On Becoming a Psychotherapist*, Windy Dryden says that many people are drawn towards a therapeutic profession because they have experienced severe personal difficulties. Very many decide to train as therapists after they feel they have been helped themselves by receiving effective counselling.

Some people may feel they have a natural empathy with others; some, that they gain great personal satisfaction from helping other human beings come to awareness and a more functional way of living. Veronica Stephenson, who with her business partner Clive Malcouronne, specializes in helping victims of child abuse, treats many severely disturbed people.

She says: 'People often ask us how we can cope with seeing so much human suffering all the time and not get saddened and depressed by it all. My answer to that is that we are constantly amazed by the indomitability of the human spirit. It's that which keeps us going, the awareness that so many people are such survivors, that they have come through horrific experiences and still have large amounts of humour, love and enjoyment of life.

'Having said that, it's important for both Clive and myself to keep monitoring what we do, to discuss our cases and to keep having therapy ourselves.'

Other counsellors have said that they gain great satisfaction from seeing people change in front of their eyes, and substituting the real self for the false one which has been assumed over the years. 'The outcome of any adequate therapy,' says Windy Dryden, 'is autonomy and the taking of personal power. There is no way that manipulation can produce genuine autonomy, and when people have finished counselling, they have worked towards irreversible and liberating changes in themselves.'

On a more practical footing, there is no age limit to becoming a counsellor. It is something which can be done at any age and taken up at any age. There is no statutory retirement age for counsellors and many people come to the profession in their forties, fifties and even sixties. Unlike many modern professions, where youth and thrusting energy are the prime qualifications, in order to be an effective counsellor you need to have experience of life, to be able to look back and see your own life in perspective and view the patterns and the changes in an objective, detached and non-judgmental way. It is not possible for those who have not worked on themselves to become effective counsellors – and often, the motivation may be simply a wish to pass on what has been learned.

The job can undoubtedly be satisfying but it is no easy ride. Clive Malcouronne says that often, he can see clients regressing back into their old ways as they board the train home.

'They seem to make such progress,' he said. 'They come to our centre terrified and withdrawn, then after a week or two they start to blossom. Often, we feel we are really getting somewhere and then we can see the postivity fading, like a battery nearing the end of its life. They get a recharge here – but it doesn't always last.'

All counsellors have to be prepared for this – most people who feel a need for counselling are in some kind of severe trouble and it is not usually easy to help them out of it. So there are continual frustrations and blocks to be met. Clients may start to hate the counsellor, not turn up for sessions, not pay – all kinds of strange behaviour are possible when people's deepest emotions are touched. Clients may want to cling to the counsellor, fall in love, never want to finish the sessions, become obsessed, start ranting and raving.

Whatever may have motivated a person to train as a counsellor in the first place, the motivation has to be strong to continue. Anyone who becomes a counsellor with an idea of being constantly gratified by client's sweetness and smooth progress is going to be both personally disillusioned and not make a good counsellor.

Finding a Good Counsellor

As should now be clear, if you are considering going to a counsellor, particularly one in private practice, ensure that they are thoroughly trained. Qualifications, though, are not everything and some of the best counsellors may have few formal qualifications but a great deal of experience. But besides training and experience, there are other factors to consider in finding the right counsellor for you, some of them of practical importance.

Do you want a male or female counsellor? This may not be an issue for you but some people may feel strongly that they can talk more easily to a woman than to a man, or vice versa, about their problem, that a counsellor of their own gender will have more understanding and insight. Having said that, most counsellors are women and if you go for counselling at a counselling centre or similar organization, you may find that you have no choice. (On a recent counsellor training course, run by Jenny Bateman, there were thirty women and six men, and this is a standard ratio.)

If your difficulties centre on homosexuality, you may prefer to consider a counsellor of the same sexual preference. Or you may want someone from your own cultural background, and someone who is of similar age. There are various organizations that offer help to minority groups and people with specific problems (see the Sources Directory) but it is worth remembering that all counsellors who go through recognized training courses will have been subjected to searching self-analysis and should be open to the difficulties of individuals from wherever they come.

On a more practical level, you need to find a counsellor who is within travelling reach of you and who you can

afford. Ask around – your GP is an obvious starting point –
for recommendations of private counsellors and counselling organizations. Libraries should also be able to provide
information about local agencies that can help. *The Counselling and Psychotherapy Resources Directory*, published
annually by the BAC, lists individuals and organizations
according to regions, with details of the kind of practice
and charges; or you can contact the BAC directly for
information.

Private counsellors often have a sliding scale for fees and
charges can vary - the higher the fees doesn't necessarily
mean the better the counsellor. Currently, fees per session
are likely to be in the range of £12 to £30. Many
organizations also have a sliding scale for fees and may
make a minimal charge for the unwaged. Some will ask for
contributions, where you give what you feel you can
afford, while many charities, voluntary organizations and
self-help groups charge no fees at all. Examples are BACUP
(British Association of Cancer United Patients) and Brook
Advisory Services, which advise young people on contra-
ception, unwanted pregnancy and personal and emotional
problems. Many counselling services offered by churches
and religious organizations make no charge; and many,
among them Relate, will not turn anybody away for lack of
funds.

If you are not sure about any particular counsellor, you
can check with the BAC whether the counsellor is a
member of BAC and works by its code of ethics.

You can similarly check whether private counsellors or
groups are BAC-accredited or whether the training courses run by a counselling organization you are considering
going to are BAC-accredited. If not, it doesn't mean they
are no good but accreditation does give some safeguard. In
any case, check what the position is about training and
supervision and, finally, follow your instincts.

Source Directory

A comprehensive resources section would run to several hundred pages; the organizations listed here are the main ones that offer general counselling and a selection of those offering help of a specific kind. If you contact a main organization or the headquarters of specialist concerns, they should be able to give you information about local counsellors and groups. There are also counselling directories available, of which the best for finding individual counsellors is *The Counselling and Psychotherapy Resources Directory*, published annually by the British Association for Counselling. This also gives invaluable details of Regional counselling organizations.

General Counselling

The British Association for Counselling
1 Regent Place,
Rugby,
Warks CV21 2PJ
Tel: 0788 578328
For general information on counselling and private counsellors and counselling organizations throughout Britain.

Mind
22 Harley Street,
London W1N 2ED
Tel: 071 637 0741
The National Association for Mental Health, with many regional offices, some providing counselling services or able to give information on local counsellors.

The Westminster Pastoral Foundation
23 Kensington Square,
London W8 5HN
Tel: 071–937 6956
Offers counselling based on the psychodynamic model for all kinds of emotional problems: bereavement, epilepsy, sex and relationship problems, serious illnesses, homelessness, redundancy, H.V, etc. In addition, there are many centres throughout the UK affiliated to the WPF:

Alton Counselling Service
Friends' Meeting House,
Church Street, Alton, Hants
Tel: 0420 89207

Chiltern Counselling Service
Beech Grove, Orchard Leigh,
Chesham, Bucks
Tel: 0494 784706

East Sussex Counselling Service
Crowborough Hospital,
South View Road,
Crowborough, East Sussex
Tel: 08926 2223

Enfield Counselling Service
St Paul's Centre,
102a Church Street,
Enfield, Middlesex
Tel: 081 367 2333

Harrow and Wembley Counselling Service
The Lodge,
64 Pinner Road,
Harrow, Middlesex
Tel: 081 429 0761

Herts and Beds Pastoral Foundation
All Saints' Pastoral Centre,
Shenley Lane,
London Colney, Herts
Tel: 0727 26867

Ipswich Concern Counselling Centre
Gainsborough House,
20 Bolton Lane,
Ipswich, Suffolk
Tel: 0437 212788

Haslemere Pastoral Centre
The Methodist Church
Lion Green,
Haslemere, Surrey
Tel: 0428 2444

Lichfield Counselling Service
30 Tamworth St,
Lichfield, Staffs
Tel: 05432 414903

Marlow Pastoral Foundation
The Farmhouse,
52 Marlow Bottom Road,
Marlow, Bucks
Tel: 06284 2799

Northampton Pastoral Counselling Service
54 Park Avenue North,
Northampton
Tel: 0604 713767

Offington Pastoral Service
The Pastoral Centre,
Offington Park Methodist Church,
South Farm Road,
Worthing, Sussex
Tel: 0903 212275

Penarth Pastoral Foundation
34 Salop Street,
Penarth,
S. Glamorgan, Wales
Tel: 0222 709358

Sutton Pastoral Foundation
21a Cheam Road,
Sutton, Surrey
Tel: 081 661 7869

Southampton Pastoral Foundation
Union Road,
Northam,
Southampton
Tel: 0703 639966

Wessex Counselling Service
Beckford Centre,
Warminster, Wilts
Tel: 0985 216594

Writtle Pastoral Foundation
The Mews,
29a Broomfield Road,
Chelmsford, Essex
Tel: 0245 284890

The Samaritans
National Administrative Office:
17 Uxbridge Road,
Slough.
A 24-hour phone service (see your local telephone directory for number) for anyone in difficulties to contact and talk in confidence about their anxieties

The Institute for Complementary Medicine
21 Portland Place,
London W1
Tel: 071 636 9543
The ICM has a register of counsellors and counselling courses.

Specific Types of Counselling

Abortion

British Pregnancy Advisory Service
Austy Manor,
Wootton Wowen,
Solihull, B95 6BX
Tel: 056 42 3225
Abortion counselling and pregnancy advice.

SATFA (Support After Termination for Abnormality)
Helpline: 071 439 6124

Care
The Scottish Association for Care and Support after Termination for Abnormality.
790 Crookson Road,
Glasgow G35 7TT
Tel: 041 882 6080

New Grapevine
416 St John's Street,
London EC1V 4NJ
Tel: 071 278 9147
Counselling agency for young women, offering free abortion counselling by appointment.

The Women's Therapy Centre
6 Manor Gardens,
London N7
Tel: 071 263 6200
An old-established centre offering counselling and psychotherapy in many areas for women, including post-abortion counselling.

Adoption

The Post-Adoption Centre
8 Torriano Mews,
Torriano Avenue,
London NW5 2RZ
Tel: 071 284 0555
Offers counselling for those who have adopted children.

AIDS

National AIDS Helpline
Tel: 0800 567 123
Government-funded, free and confidential information.

Terrence Higgins Trust
BM AIDS,
London WC1N 3XX
Helpline: 071 242 1010

Body Positive
PO Box 593,
London W14 0TF
Helpline: 071 373 9124

Alcohol and Drug Addiction

Alcohol Concern
305 Grays Inn Road,
London WC1X 8QF
Tel: 071 833 3471
Has directory of alcohol services in England and Wales.

SCODA (Standing Committee on Drug Abuse)
1–4 Hatton Place,
London EC1N 8ND
Tel: 071 430 2341
Directory of where to get help for drug problems.

The St Joseph's Centre for Addiction
Holy Cross Hospital,
Hindhead Road,
Haslemere,
Surrey GU27 1NQ
Tel: 0428 656517
Offers a comprehensive range of services for those dependent on drugs or alcohol and also their families.

The Chemical Dependency Centre
11 Redcliffe Gardens,
London SW10 9BG
Tel: 071 352 2552
Offers individual counselling and assessment and a referral service.

Tranxcall
PO Box 440,
Harrow,
Middlesex.
Information on tranquillizer addiction. Written enquiries only; send large sae for details.

Arbours Consultation Service
6 Church Lane,
London N8 7BU
Tel: 081 348 6466/7646
Offers a low-cost psychotherapy and counselling service where patients are seen by student psychotherapists under supervision. Suitable for people already attending self-help groups for chemical addiction.

Bereavement

Cruse
Cruse House,
126 Sheen Road,
Richmond,
Surrey TW9 1UR
Tel: 081 940 4818/9047
Counselling and practical advice for the bereaved.

National Association of Bereavement Services
68 Chalton Street,
London NW1 1JR
Tel: 071 388 2153
Information on local bereavement services.

Cancer Counselling

The Bristol Cancer Help Centre,
Grove House,
Cornwallis Grove,
Bristol BS8 4PG
Tel: 0272 743216

New Approaches to Cancer
The Seekers Trust,
Addington Park,
Maidstone, Kent.
Tel: 0732 848336

BACUP
121/123 Charterhouse Street,
London EC1M 6AA
Tel: 071 608 1661

Cancerlink
46 Pentonville Road,
London N19HF
Tel: 071 833 2451

The Centre for Attitudinal Healing
PO Box 638,
London SW3 4LN
Tel: 071 235 6733
Support groups and counselling for those facing serious illness.

Eating Disorders

The Vector Centre for Eating Disorders
12 Boscastle Road,
London NW5

The Eating Disorders Association
Sackville Place,
44 Magdalen Street,
Norwich NR3 1JE
Tel: 0603 621414
Telephone helpline and individual counselling.

Endometriosis

Endometriosis Society
65 Holmdene Lane,
London SE24 6LD
Tel: 071 737 4764 (evgs)

Epilepsy

Helpline: 0345 089599

Gay and Lesbian Counselling

London Lesbian and Gay Switchboard
BM Switchboard,
London WC1N 3XX
Tel: 071 837 7324
A counselling and referral service, staffed entirely by gay people.

The Pink Practice
BCM Pink Practice,
London WC1N 3XX
Tel: 081 809 7218
Help for lesbians and gay men, for individuals, couples and
families.

Lesbian and Gay Christian Helpline
Oxford House,
Derbyshire Street,
London E2 6HG,
Tel: 071 739 1249
Offers qualified counselling.

Infertility

National Association for the Childless
318 Summer Lane,
Birmingham B19 3RL
Tel: 021 359 4887

British Infertility Counselling Association
Institute of Obstetrics and Gynaecology,
Hammersmith Hospital,
Du Cane Road,
London W12 0HS

Marital and Relationship Problems

Relate
Herbert Gray College,
Little Church Street,
Rugby CV21 3AP
Tel: 0788 73242
The former Marriage Guidance organization, with many local branches, offering individual and couple counselling, also group counselling. See your local telephone directory for the nearest branch.

Miscarriage

The Miscarriage Association
18 Stoneybrook Close,
West Bretton,
Wakefield, WF4 4TP
Tel: 0924 85515

The Stillbirth and Neonatal Death Association
28 Portland Place,
London W1N 4DE
Tel: 071 436 5881

Psychic Counselling

The College of Psychic Studies,
16 Queensbury Place,
London SW7 2EB
Tel: 071 589 3292

Spiritualist Association of Great Britain
33 Belgrave Square,
London SW1X 8QL
Tel: 071 235 3351

Rape

London Rape Crisis Centre
PO Box 69,
London WC1X 9NJ
Tel: 071 837 1600

Redundancy

FOCUS (Forum for Occupational Counselling and Unemployment Services Limited)
Northside House,
Mount Pleasant,
Barnet EN4 9EB
Tel: 081 441 9300
No fees are charged to individuals, only companies.

Human Perspective Ltd
1 Russell Street,
London WC2B 5JD
Tel: 081 349 9399.
Executive counselling for redundancy and pre-retirement.

Sexual Problems

Institute of Psychosexual Medicine
11 Chandos Street,
London W1M 0EB
Tel: 071 580 1043
Can put you in touch with a local therapist.

Portman Clinic
8 Fitzjohn's Avenue,
London NW3 5NA
Tel: 071 794 8262
Specializes in help for serious sexual problems including perversions and criminal sexual acts.

Shoplifting

Crisis Counselling for Alleged Shoplifting:
081 202 5787; 071 722 3685. Evening helpline: 081 958 8859
Receives around 2500 calls a year from people who have been caught shoplifting, or who fear they may steal something out of a shop one day.

Transsexuality and Transvestism

The Gender Dysphoria Trust,
Box M7624,
London WC1N

The Gender Trust
Helpline: 071 730 7453

The TV/TS Support Group
2 French Place,
London E1 6JB
Tel: 071 729 1466

Partners' Support Group
Helpline: 081 204 4187

Victim Support

Victim Support
Cranmer House,
39 Brixton Road,
London SW9 5DZ
Tel: 071 735 9166
Offers support to victims of crime.

Victims' Helpline: 071 729 1252
A 24-hour phone service for victims of crime; also offers face to face counselling.

Young People and Children

National Association of Young People's Counselling and Advisory Services:
17–23 Albion Street,
Leicester LE1 6GD
Tel: 0533 558763.
Has directory of services all over the UK.

Childline
Freepost 1111
London N1 0BR
Free national helpline for children in difficulties: 0800 1111

Brook Advisory Centres
153a East Street,
London SE17 2SD
Tel: 071 708 1234
Counselling for young people with relationship and sexual difficulties; for local branch, see your telephone directory.

BIBLIOGRAPHY

Black, David, *A Place for Exploration: The Story of the Westminster Pastoral Foundation*. WPF, 1991

Chaplin, Jocelyn, *Feminist Counselling in Action*. Sage, 1990

Dinnage, Rosemary, *One to One* (on psychotherapy). Viking, 1988

Dryden, Windy, and Thorne, Brian, eds, *Training and Supervision for Counselling in Action*. Sage Publications, 1991

Duck, Steve, *The Psychology of Close Relationships*, Harvester Press, 1983

Gibbs, Angelina, *Understanding Mental Health*. Which? Books, 1986

Jacobs, Michael, *Psychodynamic Counselling in Action*. Sage, 1988

Jerome, Joan, *The Lost Years: Tranquillisers and After*. Virgin, 1991

Kennedy, Eugene, *On Becoming a Counsellor*. Gill and Macmillan, 1981

Kennedy, Eugene, *Crisis Counselling: The Essential Guide for Professional Counsellors*. Gill and Macmillan, 1981

Kirsta, Alix, *Victims: Surviving the Aftermath of Violent Crime*. Century, 1988

Kovel, Joel, *A Complete Guide to Therapy*. Pelican, 1978

Kubler-Ross, Elsabeth, *Living With Death and Dying*. Souvenir Press, 1981

Masson, Jeffrey, *Against Therapy*, Fontana, 1989

Mearns, Dave and Dryden, Windy, *Experiences of Counselling in Action*. Sage, 1988

Mearns, Dave and Thorne, Brian, *Person-Centred Counselling in Action*. Sage, 1988

Neild, Larry, *Escape from Tranquillisers and Sleeping Pills*. Ebury Press, 1990.

Nelson-Jones, Richard, *Practical Counselling and Helping Skills*, Cassell, 1988

Nelson-Jones, Richard, *Human Relationship Skills: Training and Self-Help*, Cassell, 1986

Noonan, Ellen, *Counselling Young People*. Methuen, 1983

Peale, Norman Vincent, *The Positive Way to Change Your Life*. The World's Work, Ltd, 1982

Quilliam, Susan and Stevensen, Ian, *The Counselling Handbook: A complete guide to what to expect and how to get the counselling you need*. Thorsons, 1990

Skynner, Robin and Cleese, John, *Families and How to Survive Them*. Methuen, 1983

Thompson, Dr Dick and Boyes, Peter, *Portraits in Courage*. Thames Methuen, 1986

Wilde McCormick, Elizabeth, *Nervous Breakdown: A Positive Guide to Coping, Healing and Rebuilding*. Unwin Hyman, 1988

INDEX